P9-CDU-083

Brain Quest

Dear Parent,

"It's Fun to Be Smart!" That's not just our slogan, it's our philosophy. For fifteen years we've been adding a big dose of "fun" into learning—first with our bestselling Q&A Brain Quest card decks; then with all the licensed games and products bearing the Brain Quest brand; and now with BRAIN QUEST WORKBOOKS.

At Brain Quest we believe:

- All kids are smart—though they learn at their own speed.

- All kids learn best when they're having fun.

- All kids deserve the chance to reach their potential—given the tools they need, there's no limit to how far they can go!

BRAIN QUEST WORKBOOKS are the perfect tools to help children get a leg up in all areas of curriculum; they can hone their reading skills or dig in with math drills, review the basics or get a preview of lessons to come. These are not textbooks, but rather true workbooks—best used as supplements to what kids are learning in school, reinforcing curricular concepts while encouraging creative problem solving and higher-level thinking. You and your child can tackle a page or two a day—or an entire chapter over the course of a long holiday break. Your child will be getting great help with basic schoolwork, and you will be better able to gauge how well he or she is understanding course material.

Each BRAIN QUEST WORKBOOK has been written in consultation with an award-winning teacher specializing in that grade, and is compliant with most school curricula across the country. We cover the core competencies of reading, writing, and math in depth—with chapters on science, social studies, and other popular units rounding out the curriculum. Easy-to-navigate pages with color-coded tabs help identify chapters, while Brain Boxes offer parent-friendly explanations of key concepts and study units. That means parents can use the workbooks in conjunction with what their children are learning in school, or to explain material in ways that are consistent with current teaching strategies. In either case, the workbooks create an important bridge to the classroom, an effective tool for parents, homeschoolers, tutors, and teachers alike.

BRAIN QUEST WORKBOOKS all come with a variety of fun extras: a pull-out poster; Brain Quest "mini-cards" based on the bestselling Brain Quest game; two pages of stickers; and a Brainiac Award Certificate to celebrate successful completion of the workbook.

Learning is an adventure—a quest for knowledge. At Brain Quest we strive to guide children on that quest, to keep them motivated and curious, and to give them the confidence they need to do well in school . . . and beyond. We're confident that BRAIN QUEST WORKBOOKS will play an integral role in your child's adventure. So let the learning—and the fun—begin!

—The editors of Brain Quest

This book belongs to:

_____

Copyright © 2008 by Workman Publishing Company, Inc.

By purchasing this workbook, the buyer is permitted to reproduce worksheets and activities for classroom use only, but not for commercial resale. Please contact the publisher for permission to reproduce pages for an entire school or school district. With the exception of the above, no portion of this book may be reproduced—mechanically, electronically, or by any other means, including photocopying—without written permission of the publisher.

BRAIN QUEST is a registered trademark of Workman Publishing Company, Inc., and Groupe Play Bac, S.A.
It's Fun to Be Smart! is a registered trademark of Workman Publishing Company, Inc.

Library of Congress Cataloging-in-Publication Data is available.

ISBN-13: 978-0-7611-4961-3

Workbook series design by Raquel Jaramillo
Illustrations by Jamie Smith

Workman books are available at special discounts when purchased in bulk for premiums and sales promotions as well as for fund-raising or educational use. Special editions or book excerpts also can be created to specification. For details, contact the Special Sales Director at the address below.

Workman Publishing Company, Inc.
225 Varick Street
New York, NY 10014-4381
www.workman.com

Printed in the United States of America
First printing June 2008

10 9 8

Brain Quest
Pre-K
Workbook

Written by Liane Onish
Consulting Editor: Jane Ching Fung

WORKMAN PUBLISHING
NEW YORK

4

Contents

ABCs

A

Ant

Find the cards with A
and color them red.

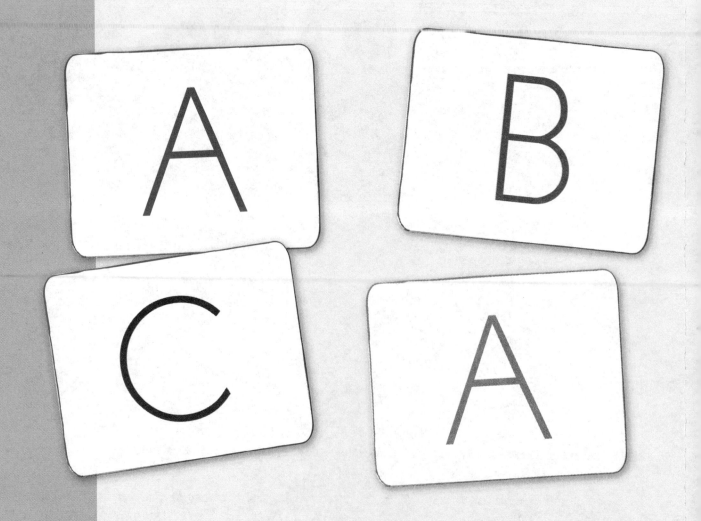

Find the cards with a
and color them **brown**.

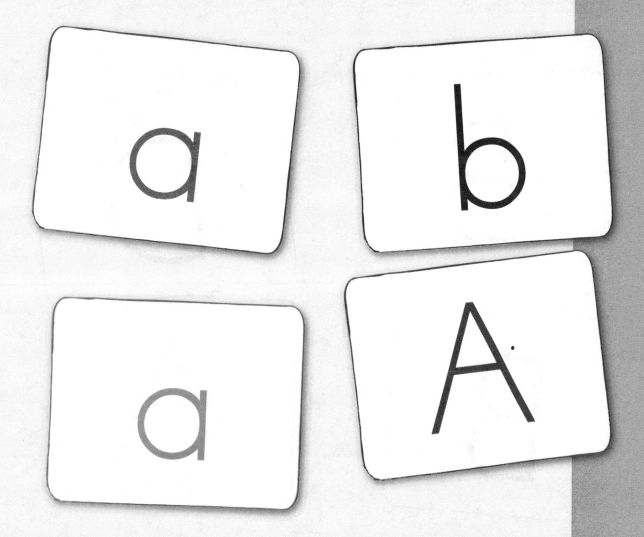

Bee

Find the cards with B
and color them yellow.

b

bee

Find the cards with b
and color them orange.

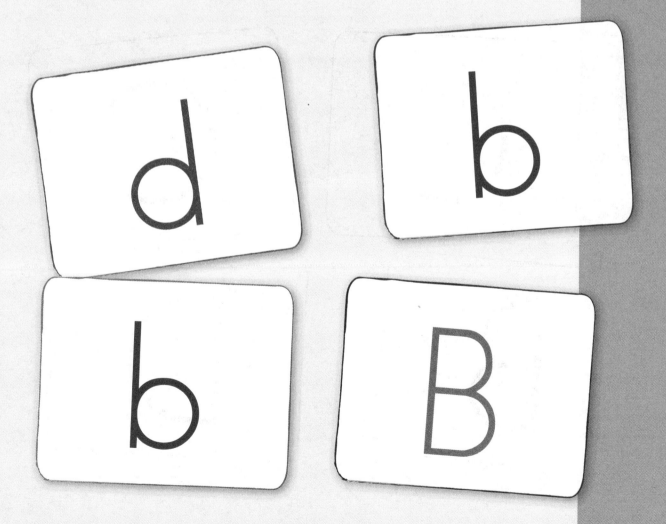

d

b

b

B

C

Cat

Find the cards with C
and color them blue.

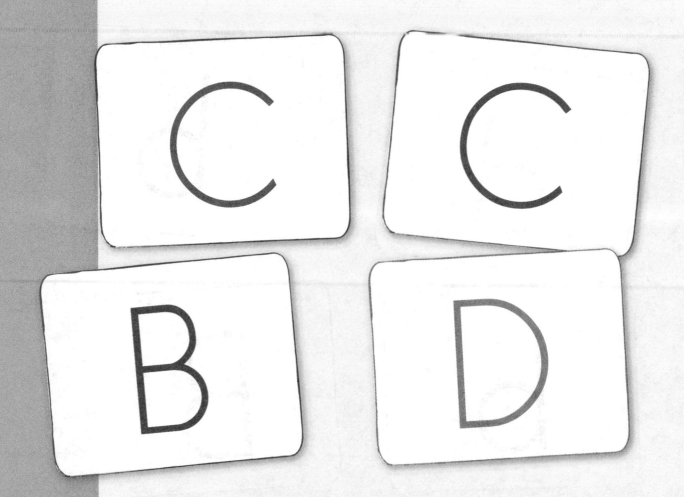

C C

B D

C

cat

Find the cards with c
and color them **purple**.

C   C

C   D

D

Duck

Find the cards with D
and color them green.

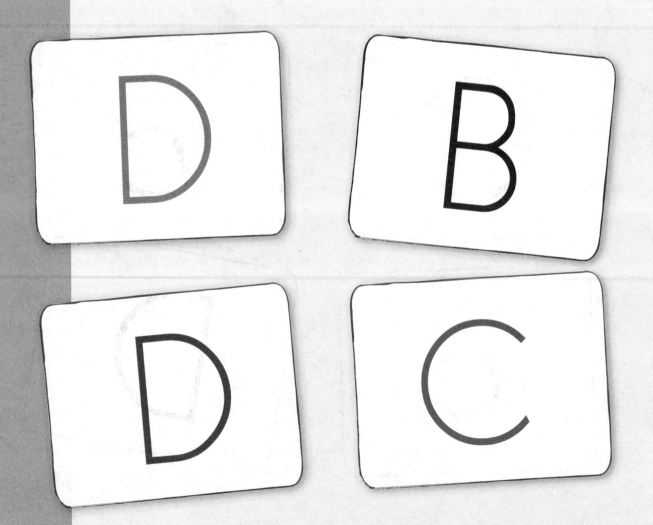

D

B

D

C

duck

Find the cards with d
and color them **brown**.

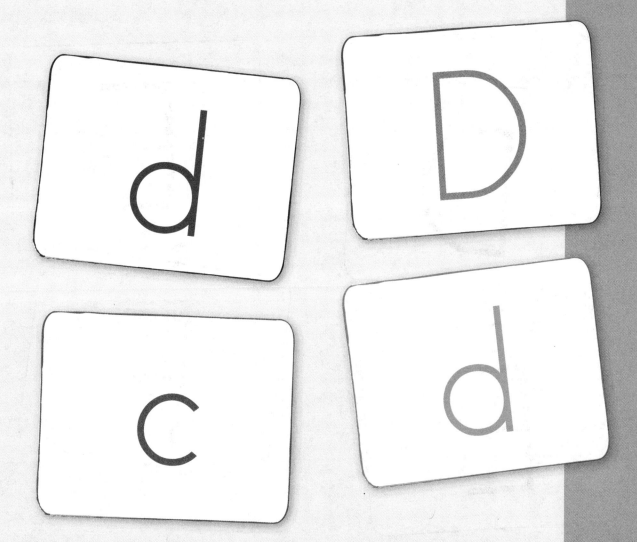

E

Elephant

Find the cards with E
and color them blue.

D

E

E

F

e

elephant

Find the cards with **e**
and color them **purple**.

f

e

E

e

F

Fish

Find the cards with F
and color them yellow.

F

F

D

E

f

fish

Find the cards with f
and color them pink.

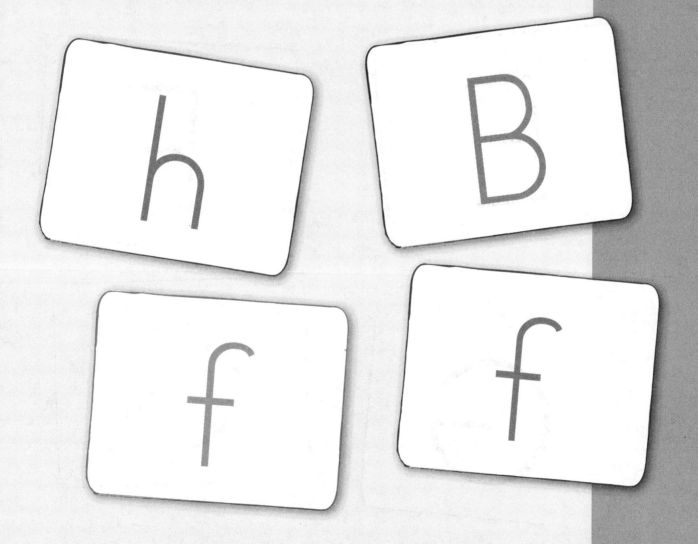

h

B

f

f

Ghost

Find the cards with G
and color them blue.

g

ghost

Find the cards with g and color them **purple**.

Match Up!

Draw a line from each capital letter to the matching lowercase letter.

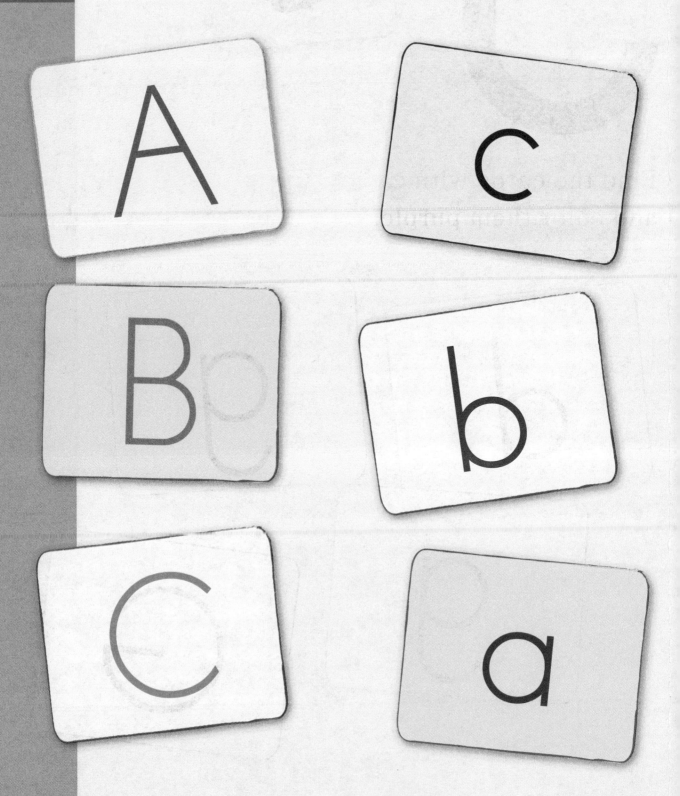

H

Find the cards with H
and color them orange.

h

Find the cards with h
and color them **red**.

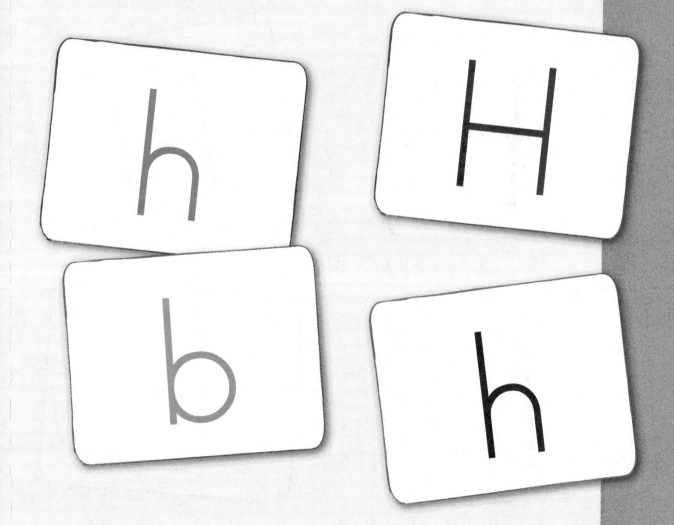

I

Igloo

Find the cards with I
and color them pink.

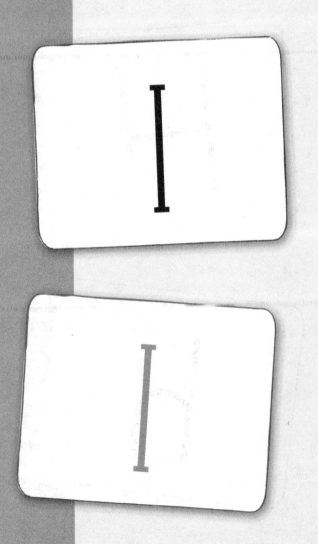

i

igloo

Find the cards with i
and color them yellow.

Jacket

Find the cards with J and color them green.

j

jacket

Find the cards with j
and color them blue.

p

j

j

m

K

Kangaroo

Find the cards with K and color them **purple**.

K

E

J

K

k

kangaroo

Find the cards with k
and color them pink.

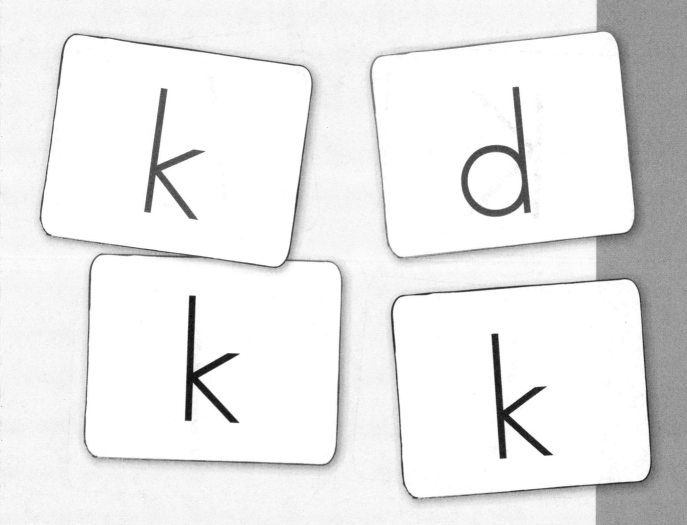

L

Lizard

Find the cards with L
and color them green.

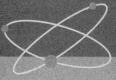

lizard

Find the cards with l
and color them **red**.

M

Mouse

Find the cards with M and color them orange.

m

mouse

Find the cards with m and
color them yellow.

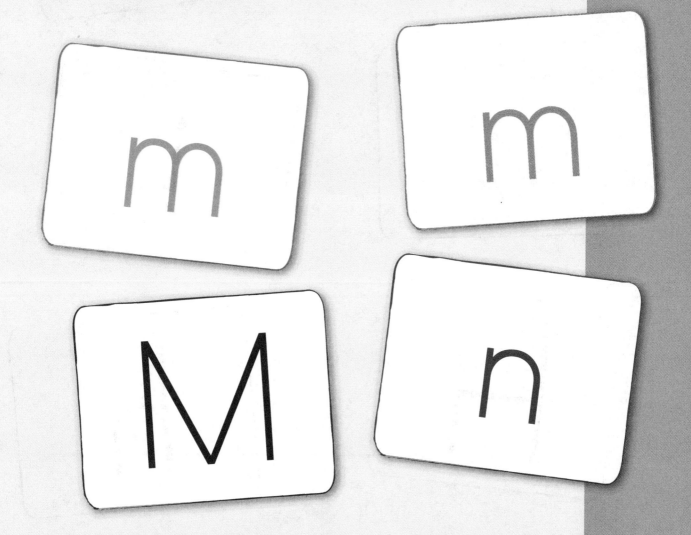

Match Up!

Draw a line from each capital letter to the matching lowercase letter.

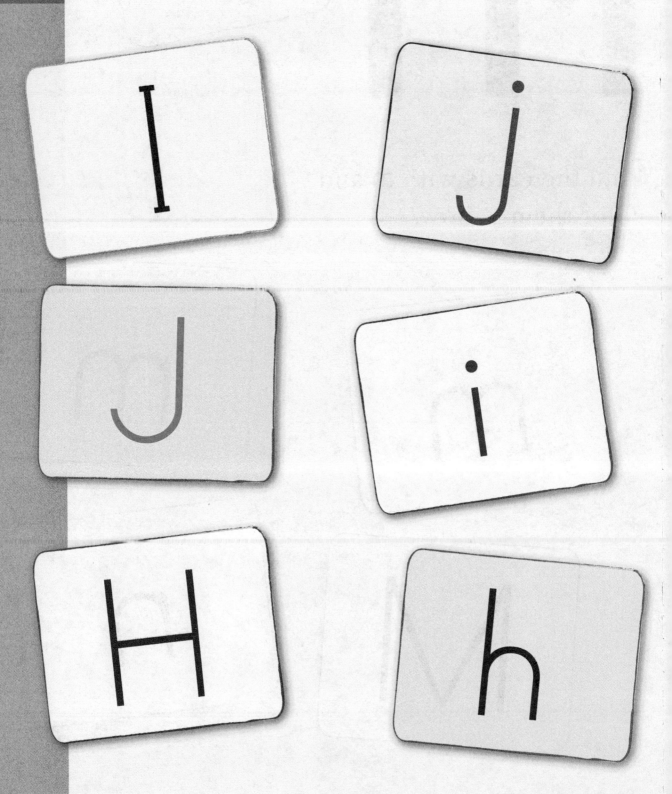

K

m

M

l

L

k

N

Newspaper

Find the cards with N
and color them **brown**.

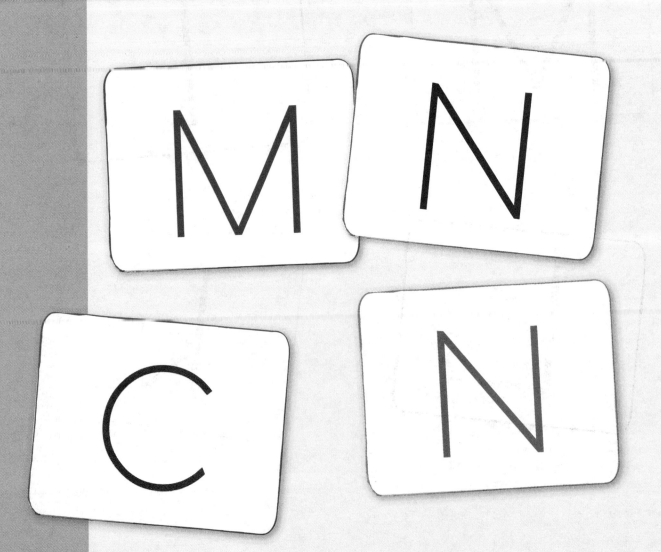

M N

C N

n

newspaper

Find the cards with n and color them **red**.

O

Octopus

Find the cards with O
and color them green.

O   N

E   O

octopus

Find the cards with o
and color them **blue**.

P

Penguin

Find the cards with P
and color them yellow.

p

penguin

Find the cards with p
and color them green.

P

p

d

p

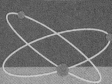

Q

Queen

Find the cards with Q
and color them **orange**.

Q   O

P   Q

q

queen

Find the cards with q and color them yellow.

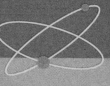

R

Rose

Find the cards with R
and color them **red**.

R R

P Q

r

rose

Find the cards with r
and color them pink.

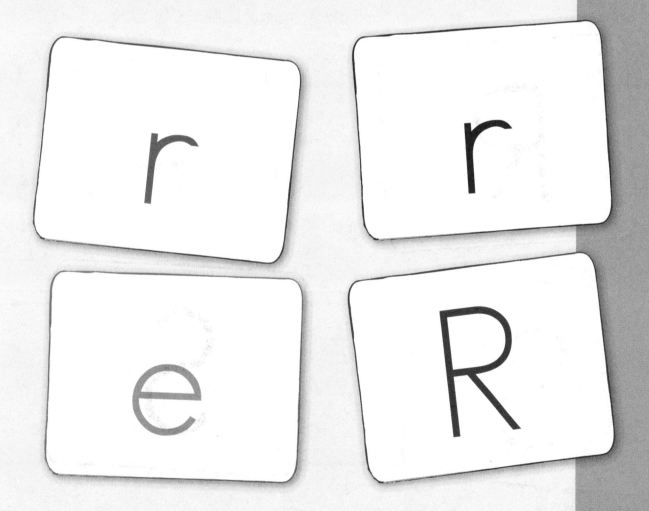

S

Snail

Find the cards with S
and color them **yellow**.

R

F

S

S

S

snail

Find the cards with **s**
and color them orange.

S   S

S   O

Match Up!

Draw a line from each capital letter to the matching lowercase letter.

Q

r

S

s

R

q

T

Turtle

Find the cards with T and color them **purple**.

T

S

T

F

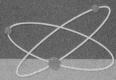

t

turtle

Find the cards with †
and color them **red**.

T   †

†   f

Find the cards with U
and color them orange.

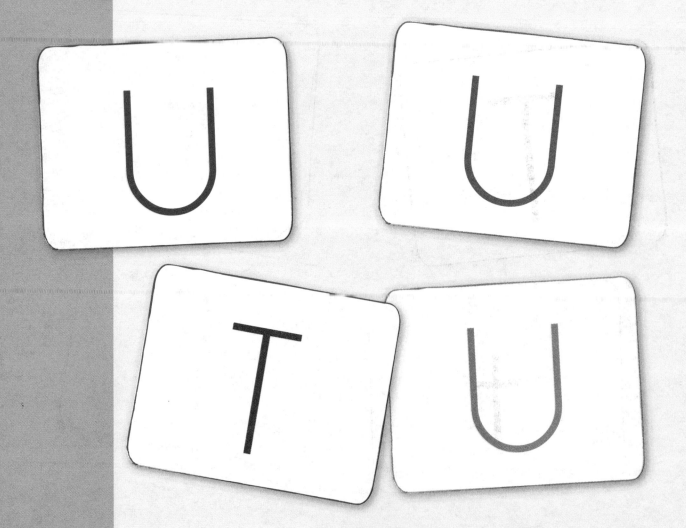

u

umbrella

Find the cards with u
and color them yellow.

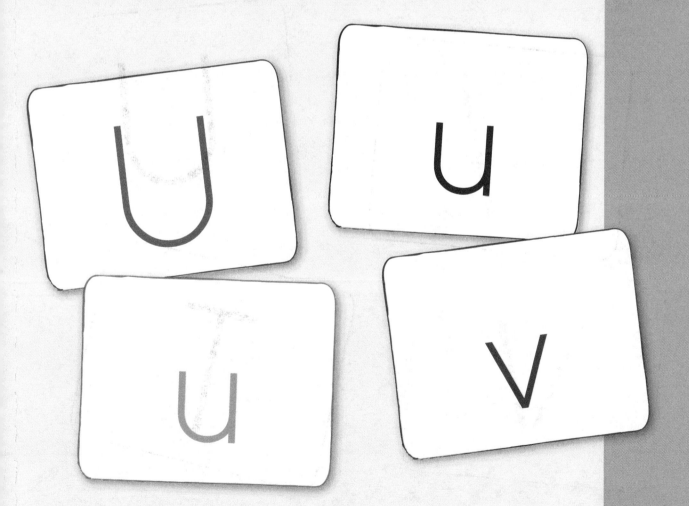

V

Violin

Find the cards with V
and color them green.

V

violin

Find the cards with v
and color them pink.

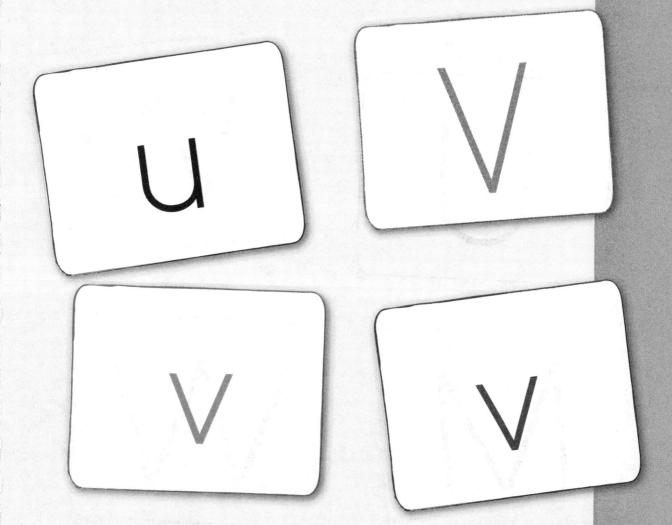

u

V

v

v

W

Whale

Find the cards with W
and color them blue.

W

whale

Find the cards with w
and color them **purple**.

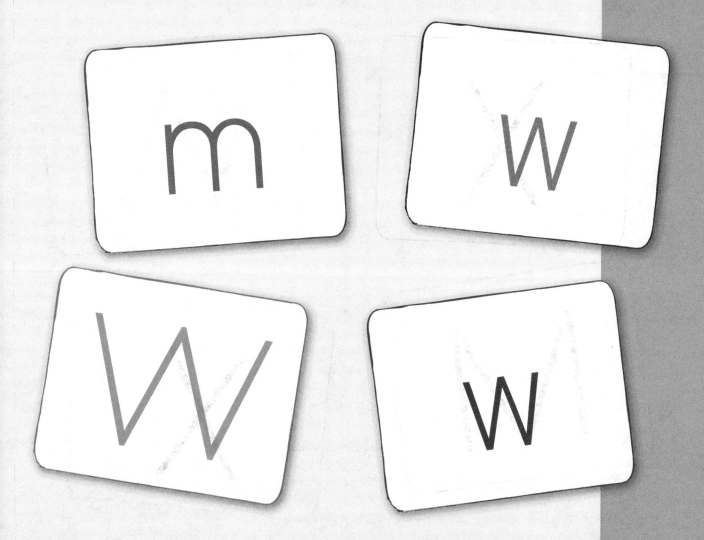

m

w

W

W

X

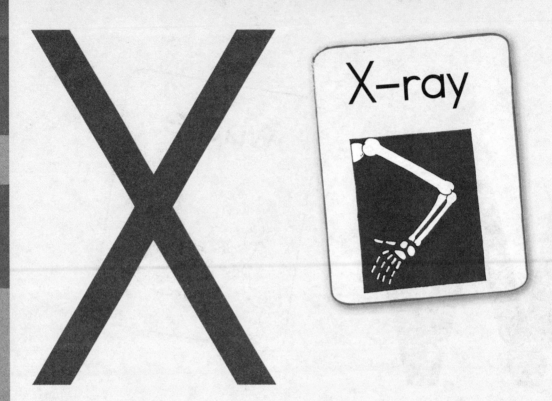

X-ray

Find the cards with X
and color them **brown**.

X

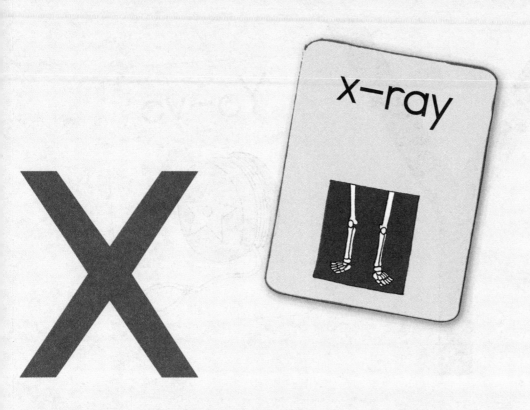

x-ray

Find the cards with x
and color them **red**.

Y

Yo-yo

Find the cards with Y
and color them orange.

y

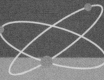

yo-yo

Find the cards with y
and color them yellow.

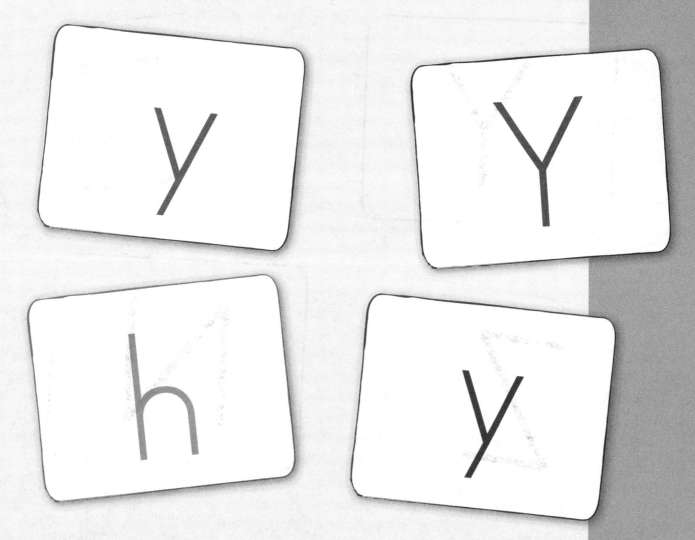

y

Y

h

y

Z

Zebra

Find the cards with Z
and color them green.

Z

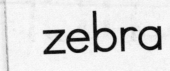

zebra

Find the cards with **z**
and color them **blue**.

Match Up!

Draw a line from each capital letter to the matching lowercase letter.

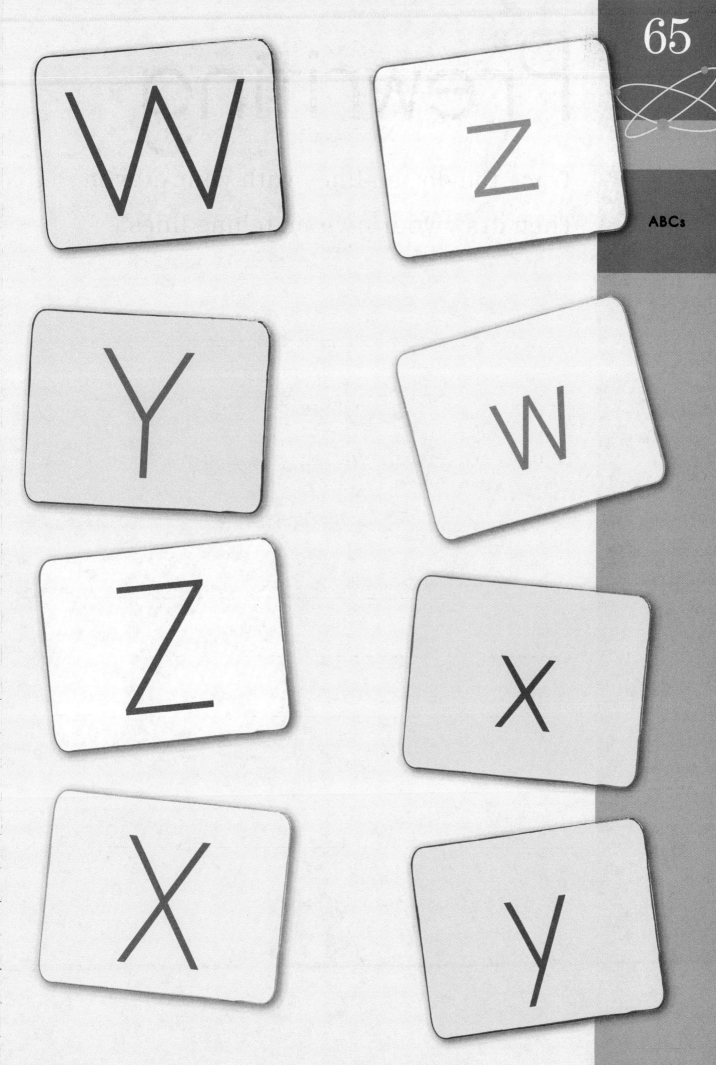

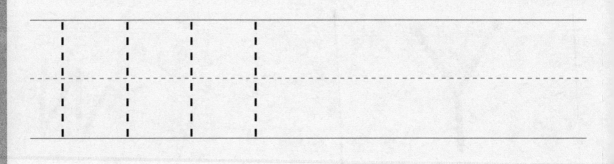

Prewriting

Trace the dotted lines with your crayon.

Then draw your own matching lines.

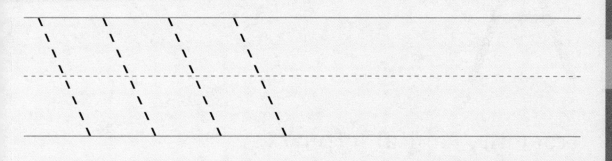

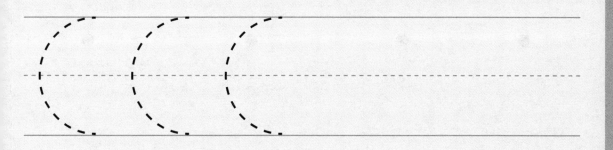

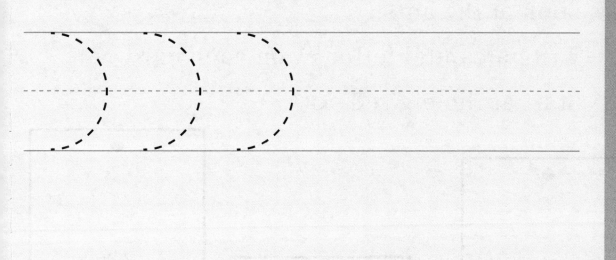

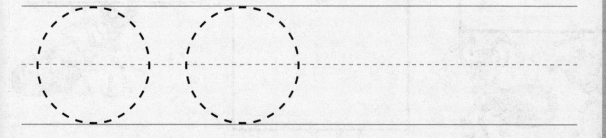

A

Trace the capital letter A.

Start at the big red dot.

Then write the capital letter A.

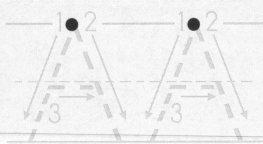

Look at the ants!

Write a capital letter A on each card.

Start at the big red dot.

a

Trace the lowercase letter a.

Start at the big red dot.

Then write the lowercase letter a.

Now write a lowercase letter a
on each card.

Start at the big red dot.

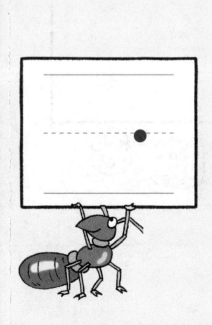

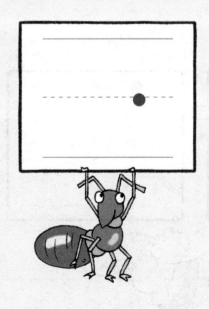

ABCs

B

Trace the capital letter B.

Start at the big red dot.

Then write the capital letter B.

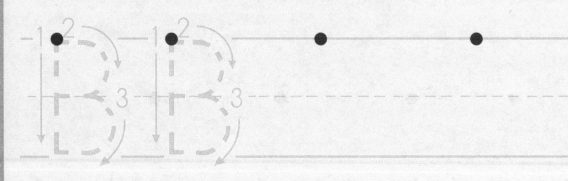

Look at the bees!

Write a capital letter B on each card.

Start at the big red dot.

b

Trace the lowercase letter b.

Start at the big red dot.

Then write the lowercase letter b.

Now write a lowercase letter b
on each card.

Start at the big red dot.

C

Trace the capital letter C.

Start at the big red dot.

Then write the capital letter C.

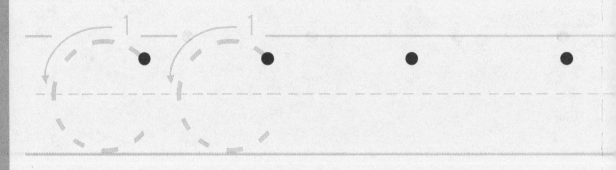

Look at the cats!

Write a capital letter C on each card.

Start at the big red dot.

C

Trace the lowercase letter c.

Start at the big red dot.

Then write the lowercase letter c.

Now write a lowercase letter c
on each card.

Start at the big red dot.

D

Trace the capital letter D.

Start at the big red dot.

Then write the capital letter D.

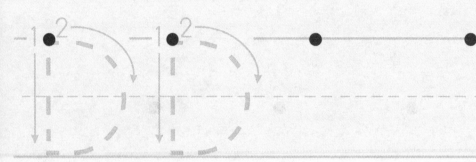

Look at the ducks!

Write a capital letter D on each card.

Start at the big red dot.

d

Trace the lowercase letter d.

Start at the big red dot.

Then write the lowercase letter d.

Now write a lowercase letter d
on each card.

Start at the big red dot.

E

Trace the capital letter E.

Start at the big red dot.

Then write the capital letter E.

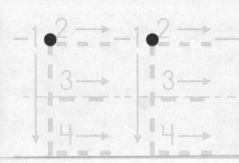

Look at the elephants!

Write a capital letter E on each card.

Start at the big red dot.

Trace the lowercase letter e.

Start at the big red dot.

Then write the lowercase letter e.

Now write a lowercase letter e
on each card.

Start at the big red dot.

ABCs

F

Trace the capital letter F.

Start at the big red dot.

Then write the capital letter F.

Look at the fish!

Write a capital letter F on each card.

Start at the big red dot.

Trace the lowercase letter f.

Start at the big red dot.

Then write the lowercase letter f.

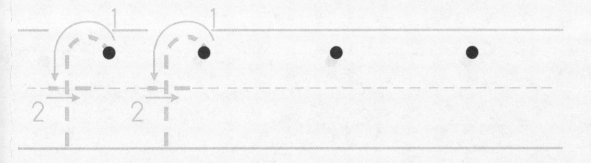

Now write a lowercase letter f
on each card.

Start at the big red dot.

G

Trace the capital letter G.

Start at the big red dot.

Then write the capital letter G.

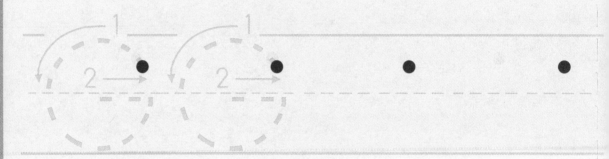

Look at the ghosts!

Write a capital letter G on each card.

Start at the big red dot.

g

Trace the lowercase letter g.

Start at the big red dot.

Then write the lowercase letter g.

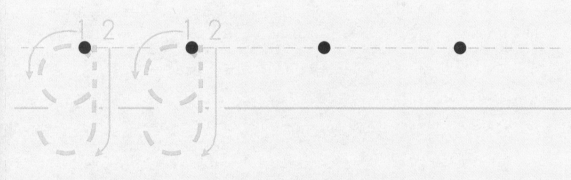

Now write a lowercase letter g
on each card.

Start at the big red dot.

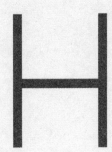

H

Trace the capital letter H.

Start at the big red dot.

Then write the capital letter H.

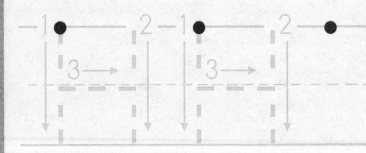

Look at the hammers!

Write a capital letter H on each card.

Start at the big red dot.

h

Trace the lowercase letter h.

Start at the big red dot.

Then write the lowercase letter h.

Now write a lowercase letter h
on each card.

Start at the big red dot.

I

Trace the capital letter I.

Start at the big red dot.

Then write the capital letter I.

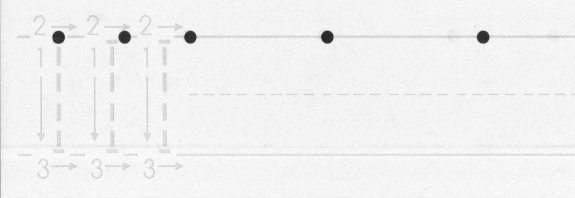

Look at the igloos!

Write a capital letter I on each card.

Start at the big red dot.

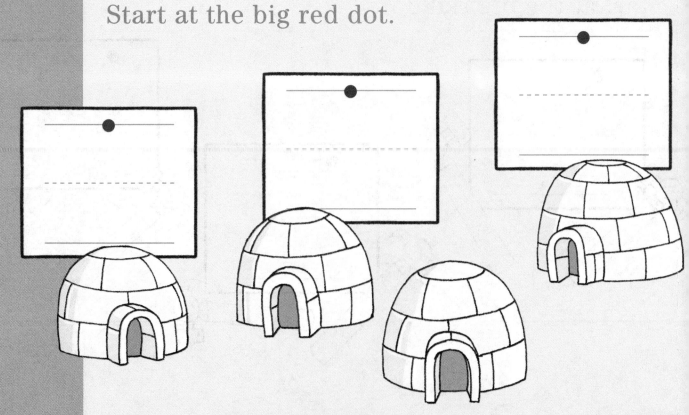

i

Trace the lowercase letter i.

Start at the big red dot.

Then write the lowercase letter i.

Now write a lowercase letter i
on each card.

Start at the big red dot.

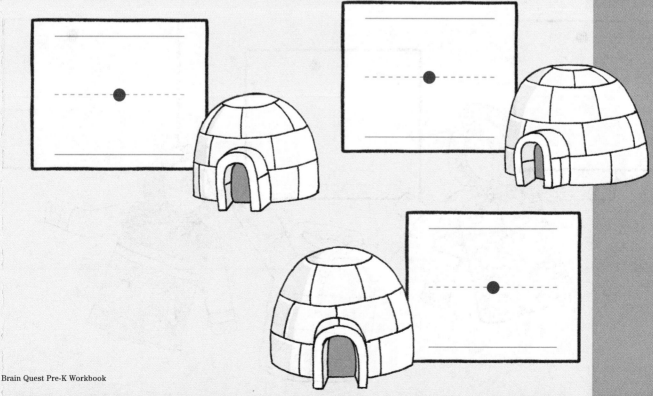

J

Trace the capital letter J.

Start at the big red dot.

Then write the capital letter J.

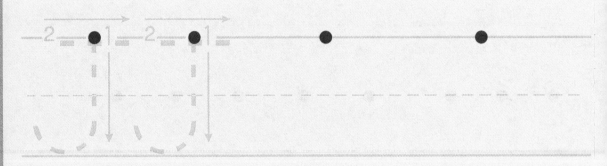

Look at the jackets!

Write a capital letter J on each card.

Start at the big red dot.

j

Trace the lowercase letter j.

Start at the big red dot.

Then write the lowercase letter j.

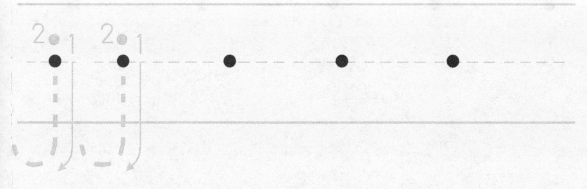

Now write a lowercase letter j
on each card.

Start at the big red dot.

K

Trace the capital letter K.

Start at the big red dot.

Then write the capital letter K.

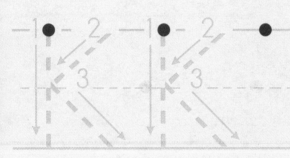

Look at the kangaroos!

Write a capital letter K on each card.

Start at the big red dot.

k

Trace the lowercase letter k.

Start at the big red dot.

Then write the lowercase letter k.

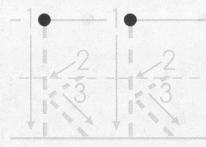

Now write a lowercase letter k
on each card.

Start at the big red dot.

L

Trace the capital letter L.

Start at the big red dot.

Then write the capital letter L.

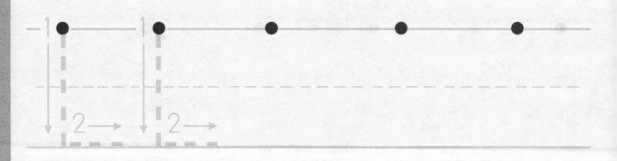

Look at the lizards!

Write a capital letter L on each card.

Start at the big red dot.

Trace the lowercase letter l.

Start at the big red dot.

Then write the lowercase letter l.

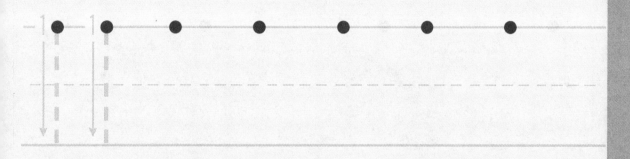

Now write a lowercase letter l
on each card.

Start at the big red dot.

M

Trace the capital letter M.

Start at the big red dot.

Then write the capital letter M.

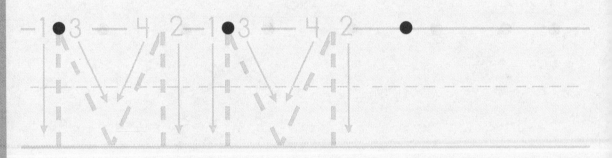

Look at the mice!

Write a capital letter M on each card.

Start at the big red dot.

m

Trace the lowercase letter **m**.

Start at the big red dot.

Then write the lowercase letter **m**.

Now write a lowercase letter **m**
on each card.

Start at the big red dot.

N

Trace the capital letter N.

Start at the big red dot.

Then write the capital letter N.

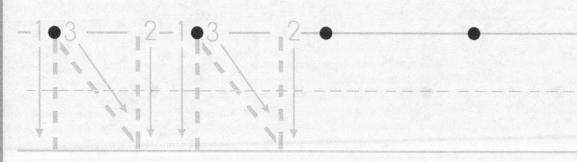

Look at the newspapers!

Write a capital letter N on each card.

Start at the big red dot.

n

Trace the lowercase letter n.

Start at the big red dot.

Then write the lowercase letter n.

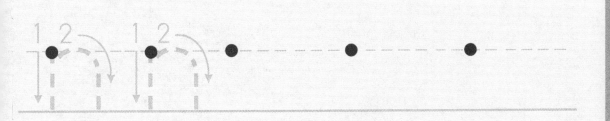

Now write a lowercase letter n on each card.

Start at the big red dot.

96

ABCs

Trace the capital letter O.

Start at the big red dot.

Then write the capital letter O.

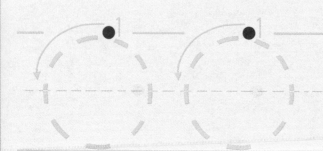

Look at the octopuses!

Write a capital letter O on each card.

Start at the big red dot.

O

Trace the lowercase letter o.

Start at the big red dot.

Then write the lowercase letter o.

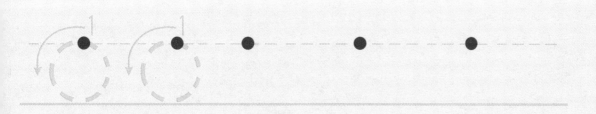

Now write a lowercase letter o
on each card.

Start at the big red dot.

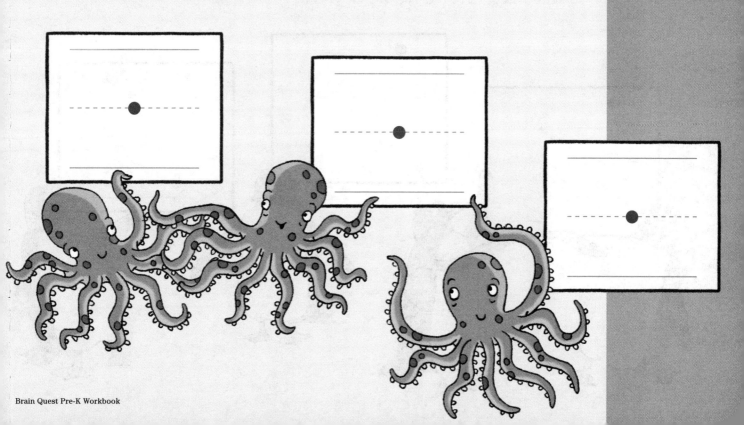

P

Trace the capital letter P.

Start at the big red dot.

Then write the capital letter P.

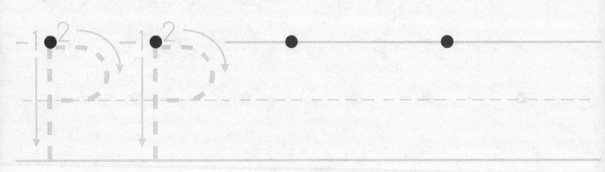

Look at the penguins!

Write a capital letter P on each card.

Start at the big red dot.

p

Trace the lowercase letter p.

Start at the big red dot.

Then write the lowercase letter p.

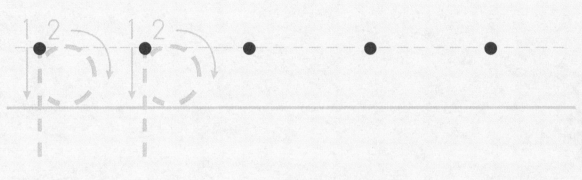

Now write a lowercase letter p
on each card.

Start at the big red dot.

Q

Trace the capital letter Q.

Start at the big red dot.

Then write the capital letter Q.

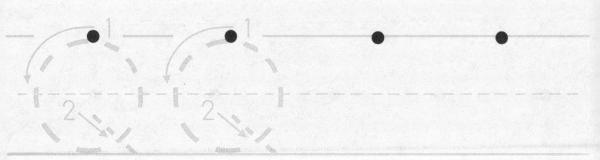

Look at the queens!

Write a capital letter Q on each card.

Start at the big red dot.

q

Trace the lowercase letter q.

Start at the big red dot.

Then write the lowercase letter q.

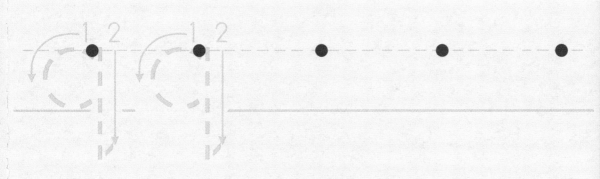

Now write a lowercase letter q
on each card.

Start at the big red dot.

ABCs

R

Trace the capital letter R.

Start at the big red dot.

Then write the capital letter R.

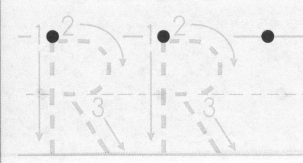

Look at the roses!

Write a capital letter R on each card.

Start at the big red dot.

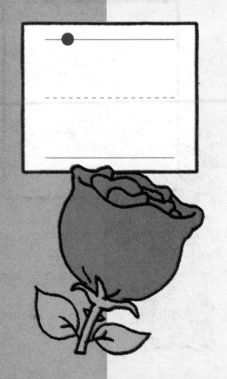
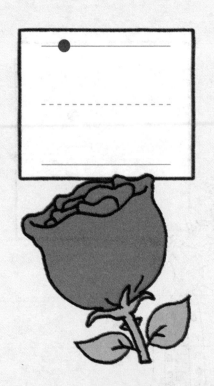
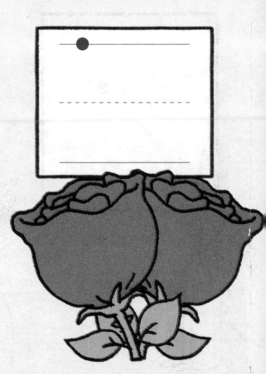

r

Trace the lowercase letter r.

Start at the big red dot.

Then write the lowercase letter r.

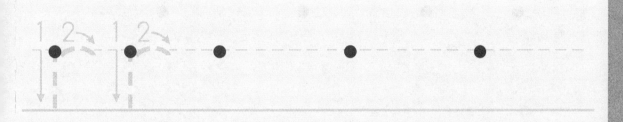

Now write a lowercase letter r
on each card.

Start at the big red dot.

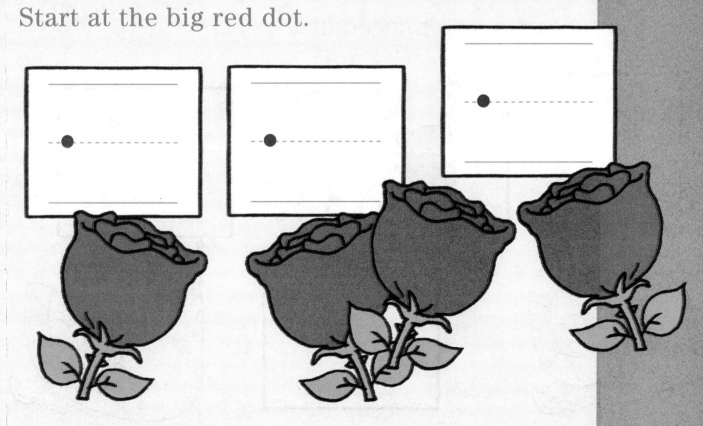

S

Trace the capital letter S.

Start at the big red dot.

Then write the capital letter S.

Look at the snails!

Write a capital letter S on each card.

Start at the big red dot.

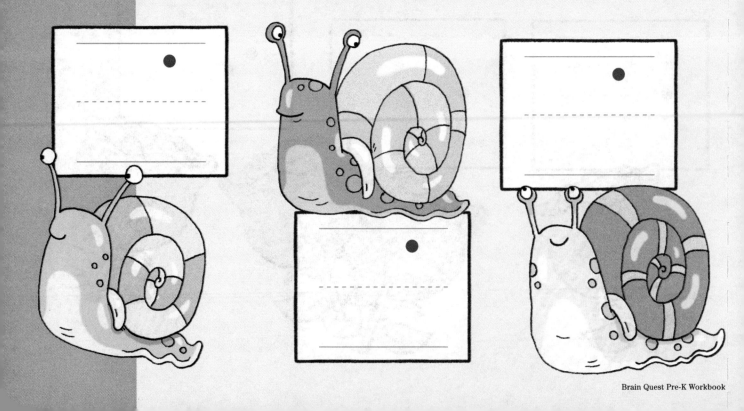

S

Trace the lowercase letter s.

Start at the big red dot.

Then write the lowercase letter s.

Now write a lowercase letter s
on each card.

Start at the big red dot.

T

Trace the capital letter T.

Start at the big red dot.

Then write the capital letter T.

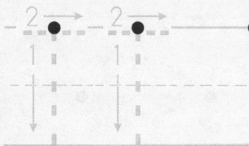

Look at the turtles!

Write a capital letter T on each card.

Start at the big red dot.

Trace the lowercase letter t.

Start at the big red dot.

Then write the lowercase letter t.

Now write a lowercase letter t
on each card.

Start at the big red dot.

U

Trace the capital letter U.

Start at the big red dot.

Then write the capital letter U.

Look at the umbrellas!

Write a capital letter U on each card.

Start at the big red dot.

u

Trace the lowercase letter u.

Start at the big red dot.

Then write the lowercase letter u.

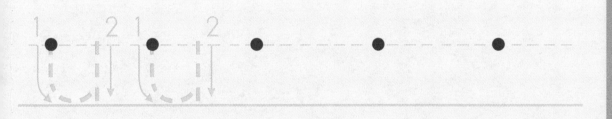

Now write a lowercase letter u
on each card.

Start at the big red dot.

Trace the capital letter V.

Start at the big red dot.

Then write the capital letter V.

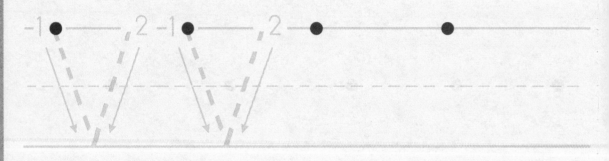

Look at the violins!

Write a capital letter V on each card.

Start at the big red dot.

V

Trace the lowercase letter v.

Start at the big red dot.

Then write the lowercase letter v.

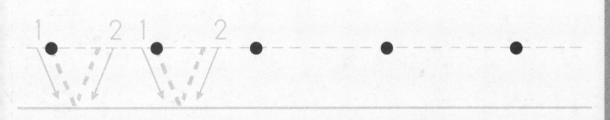

Now write a lowercase letter v
on each card.

Start at the big red dot.

W

Trace the capital letter W.

Start at the big red dot.

Then write the capital letter W.

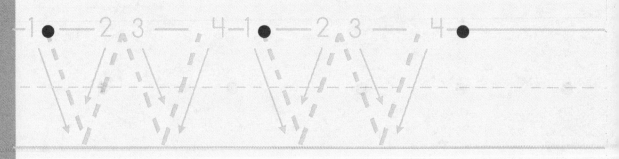

Look at the whales!

Write a capital letter W on each card.

Start at the big red dot.

W

Trace the lowercase letter **w**.

Start at the big red dot.

Then write the lowercase letter **w**.

Now write a lowercase letter **w**
on each card.

Start at the big red dot.

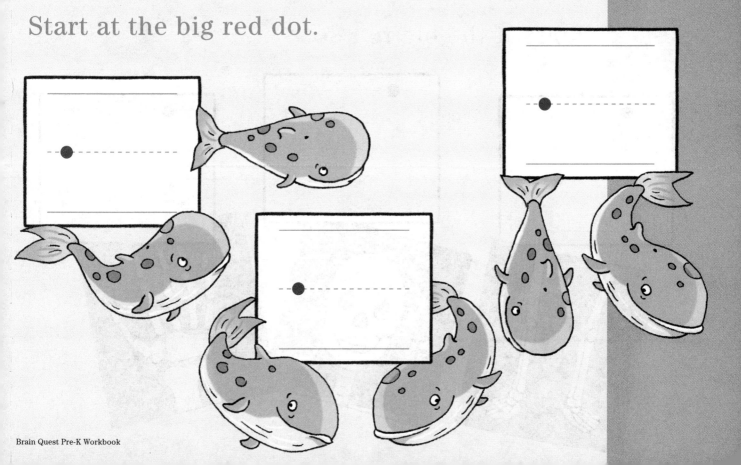

X

Trace the capital letter X.

Start at the big red dot.

Then write the capital letter X.

Look at the X-rays!

Write a capital letter X on each card.

Start at the big red dot.

X

Trace the lowercase letter x.

Start at the big red dot.

Then write the lowercase letter x.

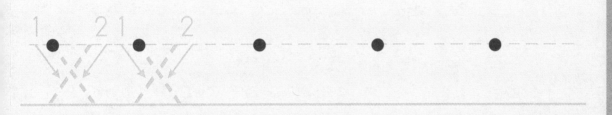

Now write a lowercase letter x
on each card.

Start at the big red dot.

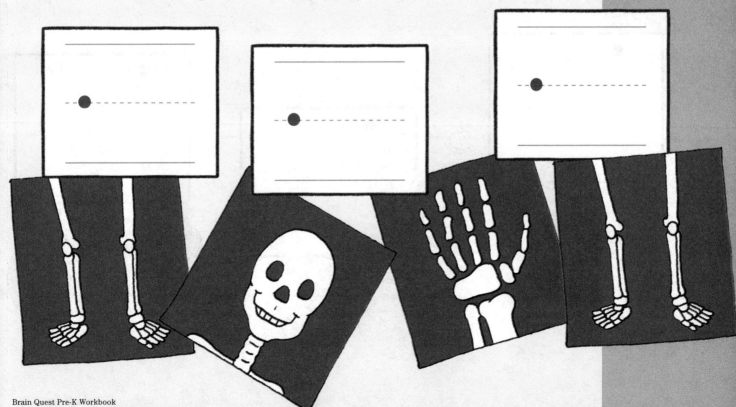

Y

Trace the capital letter Y.

Start at the big red dot.

Then write the capital letter Y.

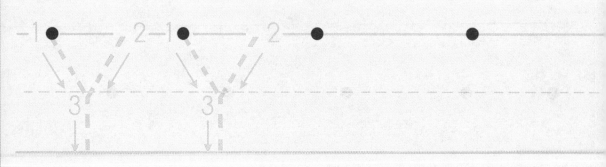

Look at the yo-yos!

Write a capital letter Y on each card.

Start at the big red dot.

y

Trace the lowercase letter y.

Start at the big red dot.

Then write the lowercase letter y.

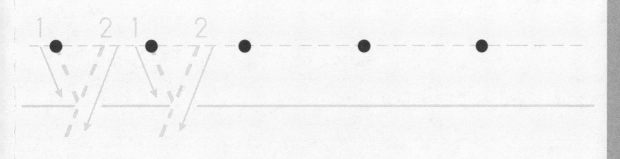

Now write a lowercase letter y
on each card.

Start at the big red dot.

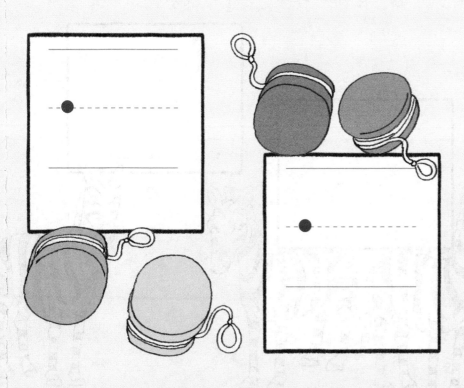

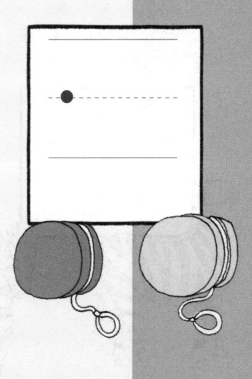

Z

Trace the capital letter Z.

Start at the big red dot.

Then write the capital letter Z.

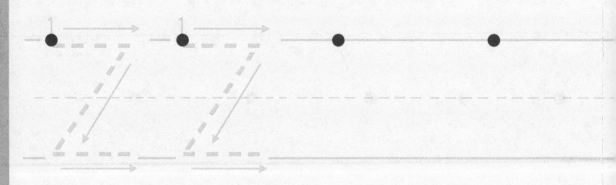

Look at the zebras!

Write a capital letter Z on each card.

Start at the big red dot.

z

Trace the lowercase letter z.

Start at the big red dot.

Then write the lowercase letter z.

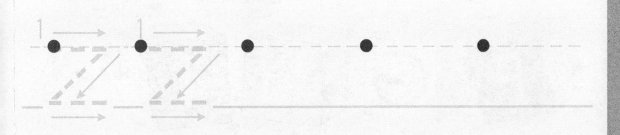

Now write a lowercase letter z
on each card.

Start at the big red dot.

Sing!

Sing the ABC song.

Point to each letter as you sing.

A B C D E
F G H I
J K L M N
O P Q R
S T U V W
X Y Z

123s

 zero

This is zero, the number 0.

0 stands for none.

Trace each 0.

Start at the big red dot.

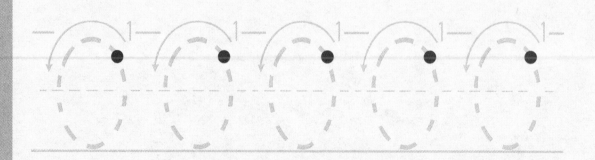

Circle the trees that have 0 apples.

one

Count the alligator on the card.

Trace each |.

Start at the big red dot.

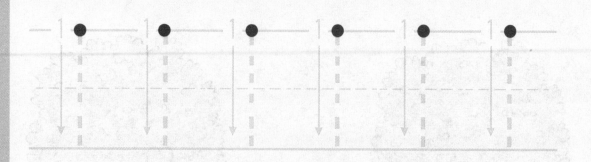

Touch and count each animal.

Circle everything that there is only | of in the picture.

2 two

Count the boots on the card.

Trace each 2.

Start at the big red dot.

Touch and count the objects in each group.

Circle the groups of 2.

3 three

Count the moons on the card.

Trace each 3.

Start at the big red dot.

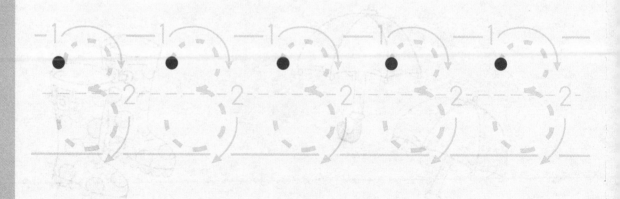

Touch and count the objects in each group.

Circle the groups of 3.

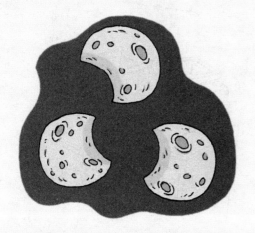

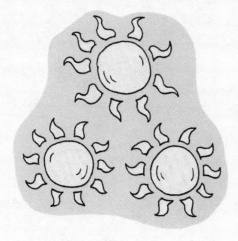

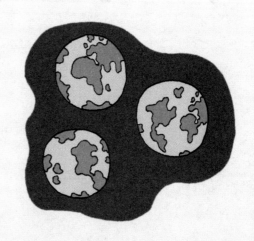

4 four

Count the trucks on the card.

Trace each 4.

Start at the big red dot.

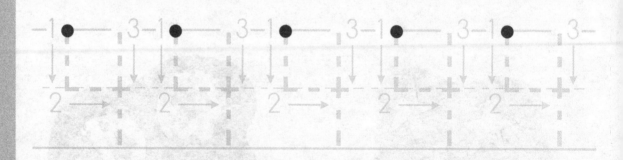

Touch and count the objects in
each group.

Circle the groups of 4.

123s

5 five

Count the turtles on the card.

Trace each 5.

Start at the big red dot.

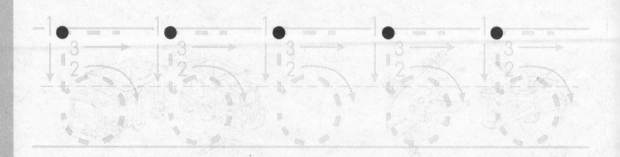

Touch and count the objects in each group.

Circle the groups of 5.

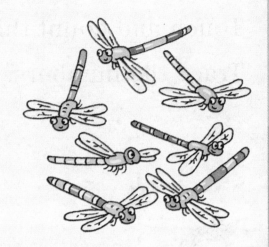

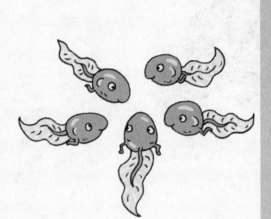

1, 2, 3, 4, 5

Touch and count the objects.

Trace the numbers.

Color!

123s

Color 1 sun yellow.

Color 2 trees green.

Color 3 clouds blue.

Color 4 flowers red.

Color 5 butterflies orange.

Brain Quest Pre-K Workbook

123s

6 six

Count the crayons on the card.

Trace each 6.

Start at the big red dot.

Touch and count the objects in each group.

Circle the groups of 6.

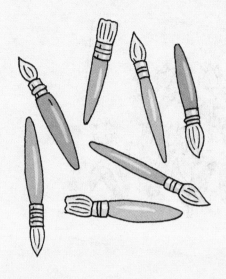

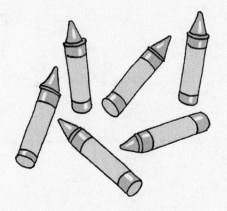

7 seven

Count the flowers on the card.

Trace each 7.

Start at the big red dot.

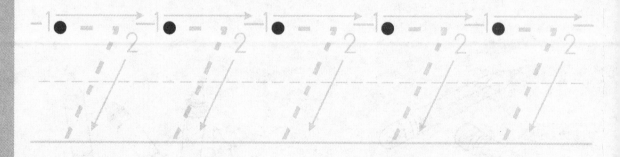

Touch and count the objects in each group.

Circle the groups of 7.

123s

8 eight

Count the fish on the card.

Trace each 8.

Start at the big red dot.

Touch and count the objects in
each group.

Circle the groups of 8.

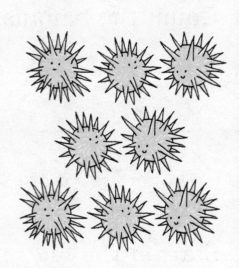

123s

q nine

Count the bananas on the card.

Trace each 9.

Start at the big red dot.

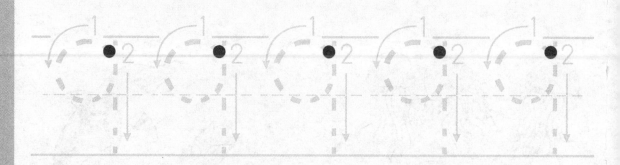

Touch and count the objects in each group.

Circle the groups of 9.

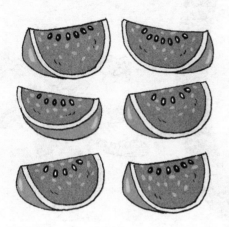

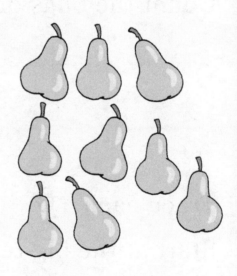

10 ten

Count the bugs on the card.

Trace each 10.

Start at the big red dot.

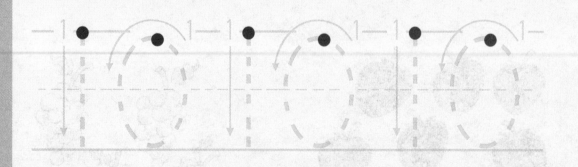

Touch and count the objects in
each group.

Circle the groups of 10.

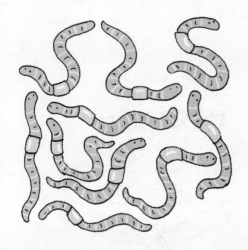

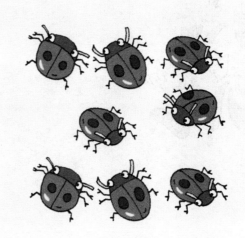

6, 7, 8, 9, 10

Touch and count the objects.

Trace the numbers.

7

8

9

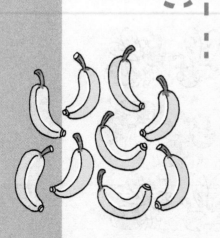

10

Music!

How many musical instruments do you see?

Draw a line from each group of instruments to the matching number.

123s

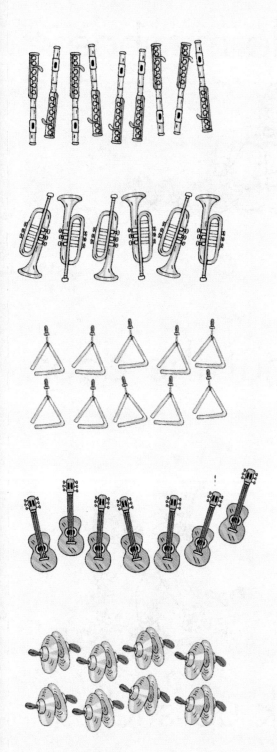

6

7

8

9

10

Buckle Up!

Trace the missing numbers as you sing "1, 2, Buckle My Shoe!"

1, 2, buckle my shoe.

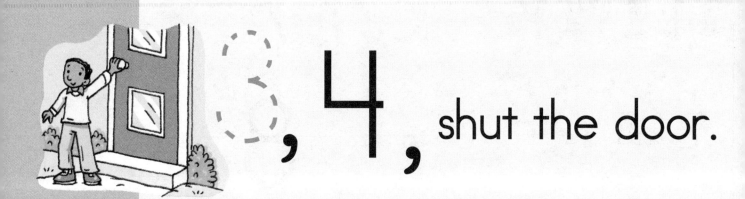

3, 4, shut the door.

5, 6, pick up sticks.

7, 8,  close the gate.

123s

9, 10, let's count again!

Now trace the numbers again.

  1 2 3 4 5

6 7 8 9 10

Dominos!

Touch and count the dots on
each domino.

Draw a line from each domino to
the matching number.

Fingers!

Count the fingers each hand is holding up.

Draw a line from the hand to the matching number.

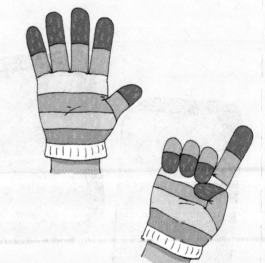

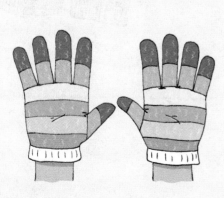

The Farm

Count the objects on each card.

Circle the cards that have the **same** number.

Berries!

Count the berries on each plate.

Circle the plate that has **fewer** berries.

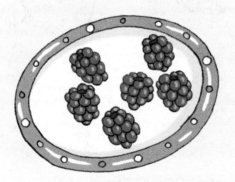 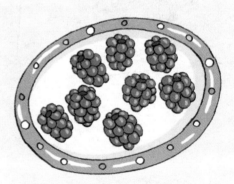

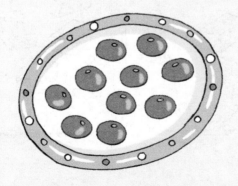 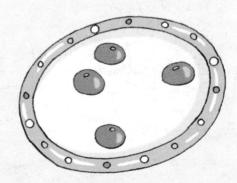

Candy!

Count the candy in each jar.

Circle the jar with **more** candy.

123s

Busy Bears!

How much does each bear have?

Circle the bear who has **more**.

123s

Phonics

A as in Ant

Say Ant.

Ant begins with the A sound.

Circle the pictures that begin like Ant.

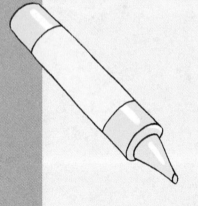

123s

0 zero

This is zero, the number 0.

0 stands for none.

Trace each 0.

Start at the big red dot.

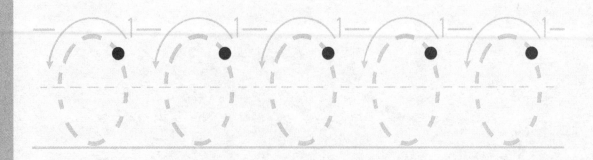

Circle the trees that have 0 apples.

| one

Count the alligator on the card.

Trace each |.

Start at the big red dot.

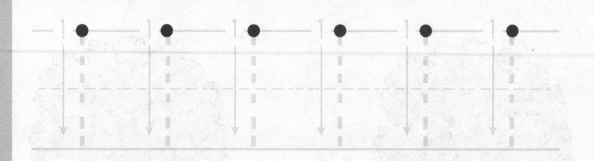

Touch and count each animal.

Circle everything that there is only | of in the picture.

2 two

Count the boots on the card.

Trace each 2.

Start at the big red dot.

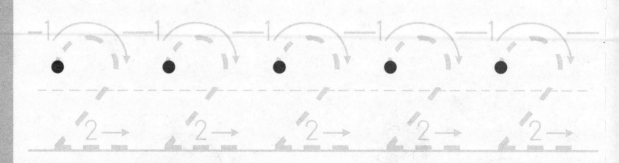

Touch and count the objects in each group.

Circle the groups of 2.

123s

3 three

Count the moons on the card.

Trace each 3.

Start at the big red dot.

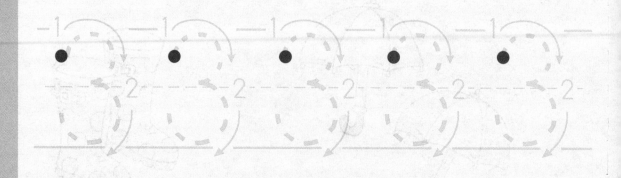

Touch and count the objects in
each group.

Circle the groups of 3.

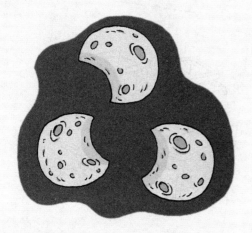

123s

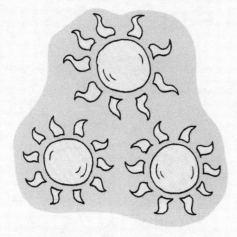

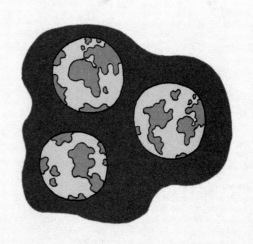

123s

4 four

Count the trucks on the card.

Trace each 4.

Start at the big red dot.

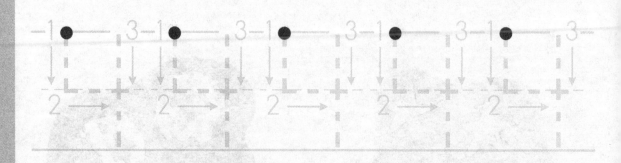

Touch and count the objects in each group.

Circle the groups of 4.

5 five

Count the turtles on the card.

Trace each 5.

Start at the big red dot.

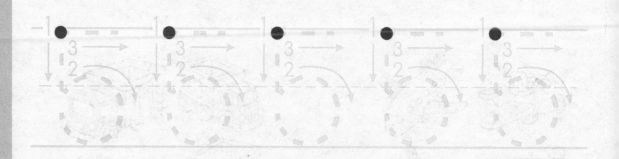

Touch and count the objects in each group.

Circle the groups of 5.

123s

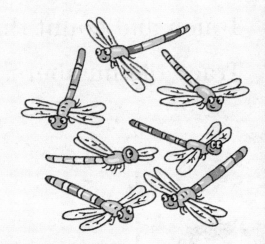

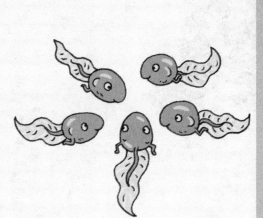

1, 2, 3, 4, 5

Touch and count the objects.

Trace the numbers.

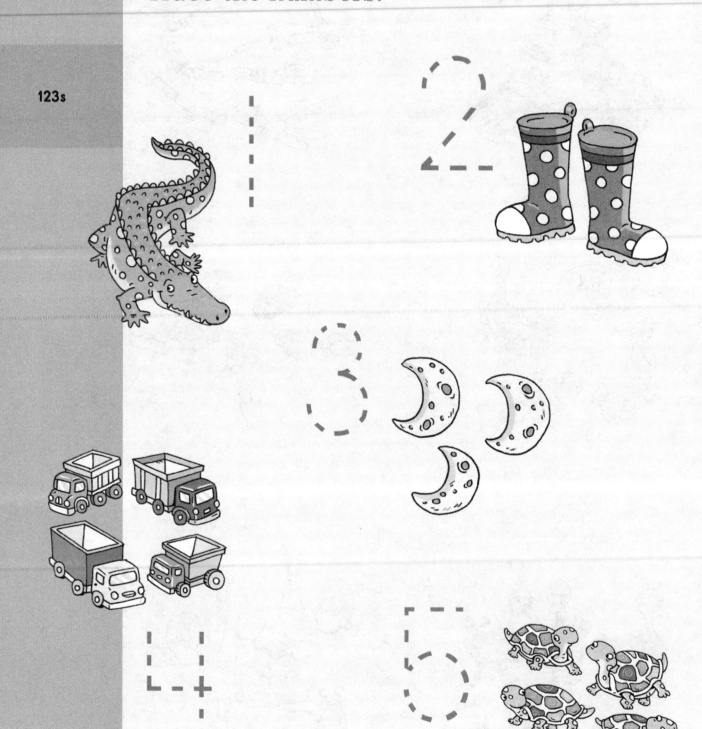

Color!

Color 1 sun yellow.

Color 2 trees green.

Color 3 clouds blue.

Color 4 flowers **red**.

Color 5 butterflies orange.

6 six

Count the crayons on the card.

Trace each 6.

Start at the big red dot.

Touch and count the objects in each group.

Circle the groups of 6.

123s

7 seven

Count the flowers on the card.

Trace each 7.

Start at the big red dot.

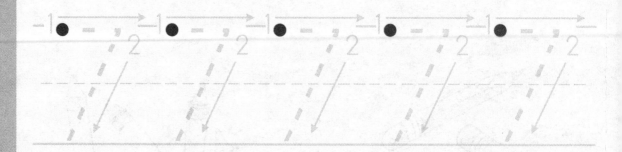

Touch and count the objects in each group.

Circle the groups of 7.

123s

8 eight

Count the fish on the card.

Trace each 8.

Start at the big red dot.

Touch and count the objects in each group.

Circle the groups of 8.

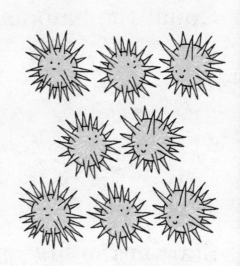

q nine

Count the bananas on the card.

Trace each q.

Start at the big red dot.

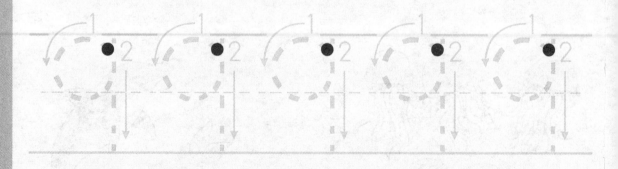

Touch and count the objects in each group.

Circle the groups of 9.

123s

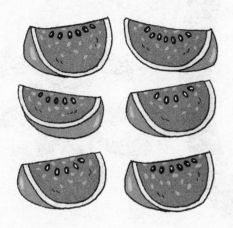

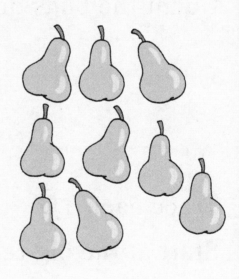

10 ten

Count the bugs on the card.

Trace each 10.

Start at the big red dot.

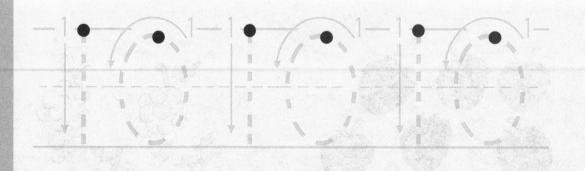

Touch and count the objects in
each group.

Circle the groups of 10.

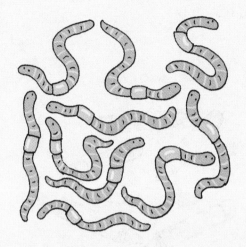

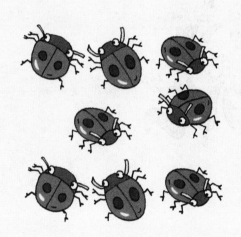

6, 7, 8, 9, 10

Touch and count the objects.

Trace the numbers.

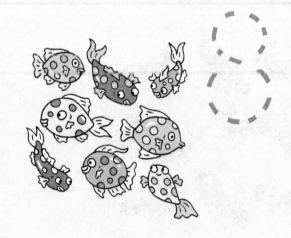

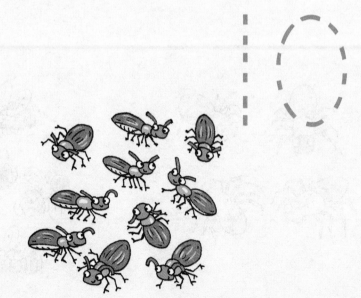

Music!

How many musical instruments
do you see?

Draw a line from each group of
instruments to the matching number.

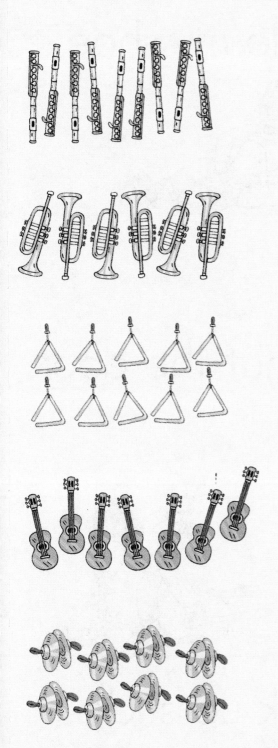

6

7

8

9

10

Buckle Up!

Trace the missing numbers as you sing "1, 2, Buckle My Shoe!"

1, 2, buckle my shoe.

 3, 4, shut the door.

5, 6, pick up sticks.

7, 8, close the gate.

9, 10, let's count again!

Now trace the numbers again.

Dominos!

Touch and count the dots on each domino.

Draw a line from each domino to
the matching number.

7

9

6

8

10

Fingers!

Count the fingers each hand is holding up.

Draw a line from the hand to the matching number.

123s

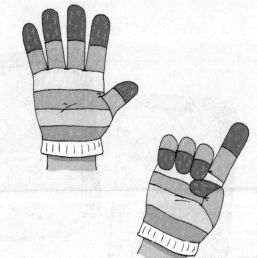

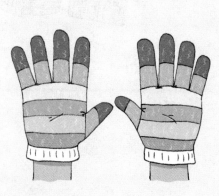

Brain Quest Pre-K Workbook

The Farm

Count the objects on each card.

Circle the cards that have the **same** number.

123s

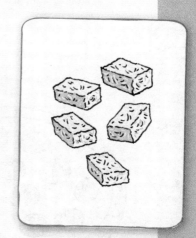

Berries!

Count the berries on each plate.

Circle the plate that has **fewer** berries.

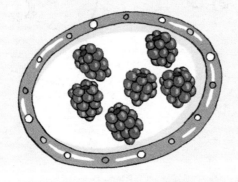 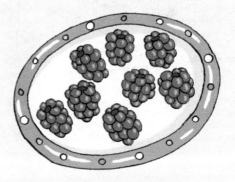

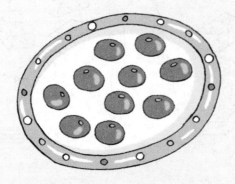 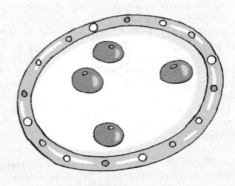

Candy!

Count the candy in each jar.

Circle the jar with **more** candy.

Busy Bears!

How much does each bear have?

Circle the bear who has **more**.

Phonics

A as in Ant

Say Ant.

Ant begins with the A sound.

Circle the pictures that begin like Ant.

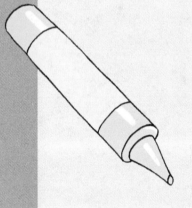

B as in Bee

Say Bee.

Bee begins with the B sound.

Circle the pictures that begin like Bee.

C as in Cat

Say Cat.

Cat begins with the C sound.

Write a capital letter C under the pictures that begin like Cat.

Phonics

_____   _____   _____

- - - - -   - - - - -   - - - - -

_____   _____   _____

_____   _____   _____

- - - - -   - - - - -   - - - - -

_____   _____   _____

D as in Duck

Say Duck.

Duck begins with the D sound.

Color the cards with pictures that begin like Duck.

E as in Elephant

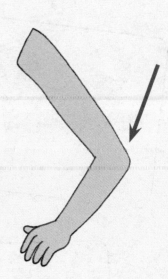

Say Elephant.

Elephant begins with the E sound.

Circle the pictures that begin like Elephant.

Phonics

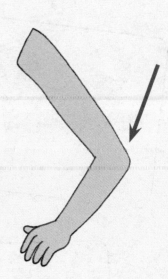

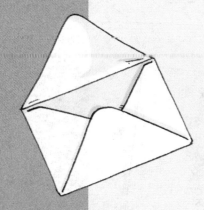

F as in Fish

Say Fish.

Fish begins with the F sound.

Circle the pictures that begin like Fish.

G as in Ghost

Say Ghost.

Ghost begins with the G sound.

Draw a line from the G to the pictures that begin like Ghost.

Phonics

G

H as in Hammer

Say Hammer.

Hammer begins with the H sound.

Circle the pictures that begin like Hammer.

Phonics

I as in Igloo

Phonics

Say Igloo.

Igloo begins with the I sound.

Write a capital letter I under the pictures that begin like Igloo.

J as in Jacket

Say Jacket.

Jacket begins with the **J** sound.

Draw a line from the **J** to the pictures that begin like Jacket.

K as in Kangaroo

Say Kangaroo.

Kangaroo begins with the K sound.

Color the cards with pictures that begin like Kangaroo.

Phonics

L as in Lizard

Say Lizard.

Lizard begins with the L sound.

Circle the pictures that begin like Lizard.

M as in Mouse

Phonics

Say Mouse.

Mouse begins with the M sound.

Write a capital letter M under the pictures that begin like Mouse.

_____

- - - - - - - - -

_____

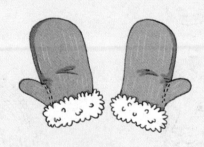

_____

- - - - - - - - -

_____

N as in Newspaper

Say Newspaper.

Newspaper begins with the N sound.

Draw a line from the N to the pictures that begin like Newspaper.

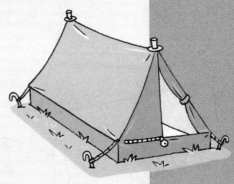

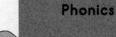

O as in Octopus

Say Octopus.

Octopus begins with the O sound.

Color the cards with pictures that begin like Octopus.

Phonics

O as in Octopus

P as in Penguin

Say Penguin.

Penguin begins with the P sound.

Circle the pictures that begin like Penguin.

Q as in Queen

Say Queen.

Queen begins with the Q sound.

Write a capital letter Q under the pictures that begin like Queen.

R as in Rose

Say Rose.

Rose begins with the R sound.

Draw a line from the letter R to the pictures that begin like Rose.

S as in Snail

Say Snail.

Snail begins with the S sound.

Circle the pictures that begin like Snail.

Phonics

T as in Turtle

Say Turtle.

Turtle begins with the T sound.

Write a capital letter T under the pictures that begin like Turtle.

U as in Umbrella

Say Umbrella.

Umbrella begins with the U sound.

Circle the picture that begins like Umbrella.

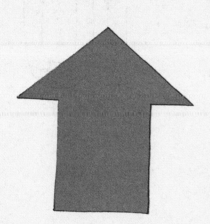

V as in Violin

Say Violin.

Violin begins with the V sound.

Color the cards with pictures that begin like Violin.

Was in Whale

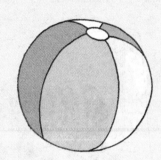

Phonics

Say Whale.

Whale begins with the W sound.

Circle the pictures that begin like Whale.

X as in X-ray

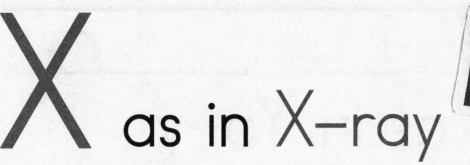

Say X-ray.

X-ray begins with the X sound.

Circle the picture that begins like X-ray.

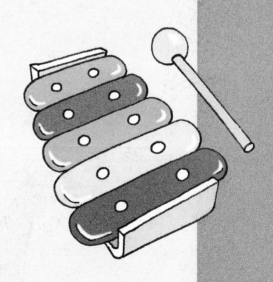

Y as in Yo-yo

Say Yo-yo. Yo-yo begins with the Y sound.

Draw a line from the letter Y to the pictures that begin like Yo-yo.

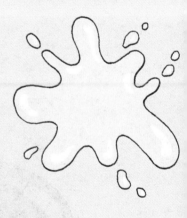

Z as in Zebra

Say Zebra. Zebra begins with the Z sound.

Write a capital letter Z under the pictures that begin like Zebra.

A to Z

Say the word for each picture.

What beginning sound do you hear?

Phonics

Vocabulary

Big

These animals are **big**.

Say the name of each animal.

Then color each picture.

Vocabulary

Small

These animals are **small.**

Say the name of each animal.

Then color each picture.

  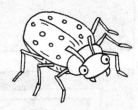

Vocabulary

What is your favorite small animal?

Draw a picture of it in the box.

Signs!

When a store is **open** you can go in and buy things. Do you see the OPEN sign? Color it green.

Vocabulary

When a store is **closed** you can't go in and
buy things. Do you see the CLOSED sign?
Color it **red**.

Traffic Lights

Traffic lights tell us what to do.

Vocabulary

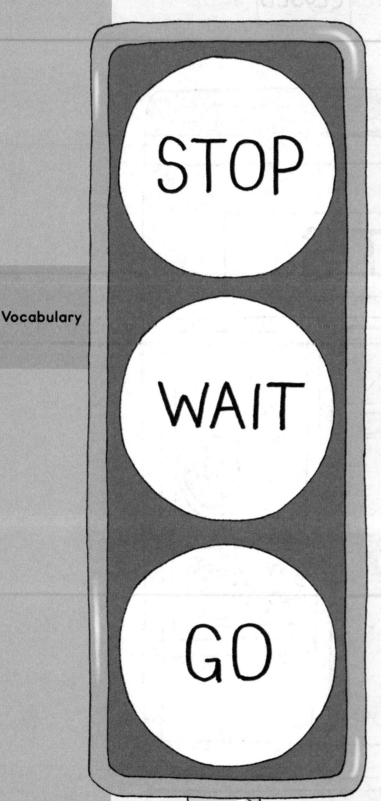

Red means STOP.
Color the light at the
top **red**.

Yellow means WAIT.
Color the light in the
middle yellow.

Green means GO.
Color the light at the
bottom green.

The cars go.

What color is
the traffic light?
Color the light.

The cars stop.

What color is
the traffic light?
Color the light.

Street Signs

Street signs help everyone stay safe.

This sign tells cars to stop.

This sign means it is safe to cross the street.

This sign means buses stop here.

Circle the sign that goes with each picture.

Vocabulary

Toy Store

Say the the name of the **toy** on each sign.

doll

car

train

boat

Draw a line from each sign to the matching toy in the store.

Vocabulary

duck

truck

bear

ball

Market!

Say the name of the **food** on each sign.

Vocabulary

eggs

milk

juice

yogurt

Draw a line from each sign to the matching food on the shelf.

onion

tomato

Vocabulary

cucumber

plum

pear

corn

apple

Let's Go!

Listen to each riddle.

Draw a line to the matching picture.

Then color the picture.

Vocabulary

Let's go up, up, and away! I fly high up in the sky. What am I?

car

You have to wear a seat belt in me. I have wheels. What am I?

airplane

"Everyone wears a life vest. We are ready to set sail!" What am I?

bus

I go "choo! choo!" I travel on a track. What am I?

sailboat

Vocabulary

I can fit more people than a car. I am a rectangle. What am I?

train

Farm Friends

Say the name of each **animal.**

What sound does it make?

Vocabulary

Shapes and Colors

Red

Color the apples **red**.

Color the wagon **red**.

Color the ice-cream bar **red**.

Can you think of something else that is **red**?
Draw it here.

Shapes and
Colors

Orange

Color the basketball orange.

Color the butterflies orange.

Color the pumpkin orange.

Shapes and Colors

Can you think of something else that is orange? Draw it here.

Shapes and
Colors

Yellow

Color the sun yellow.

Color the flowers yellow.

Color the bees yellow.

Can you think of something else that is yellow? Draw it here.

Green

Color the alligator green.

Color the leaves green.

Color the snake green.

Can you think of something else that is green? Draw it here.

Blue

Color the sky **blue**.

Color the mailbox **blue**.

Color the bluebird **blue**.

Can you think of something else that is blue? Draw it here.

Purple

Color the jelly jar **purple**.

Color the plums **purple**.

Color the violets **purple**.

Can you think of something else that is **purple?** Draw it here.

Shapes and Colors

Rainbow!

Color the rainbow.

red orange yellow green blue indigo violet

Shapes and
Colors

Tasty!

What color should each food be?

Name the food. Then color it in.

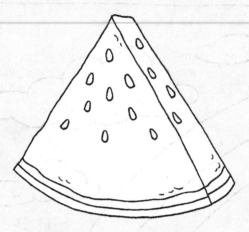

watermelon

banana

strawberry

lettuce

orange

carrot

cherry

lemon

grapes

broccoli

Circle

A **circle** is round.

Trace the circle.

Draw a face inside the circle.

Now draw your own circle
in the space below.

How many circles can you find?

Point to all the circles in the picture.

Shapes and
Colors

Rectangle

A **rectangle** has four sides.

Two sides are long. Two sides are short.

Trace the rectangle.

Draw a picture inside the rectangle.

Now draw your own rectangle
in the space below.

How many rectangles can you find?

Point to all the rectangles in the picture.

Square

A **square** has four equal sides.

Trace the square.

Draw a house using the square.

Now draw your own square
in the space below.

How many squares can you find?

Point to all the squares in the picture.

Shapes and
Colors

Triangle

A **triangle** has three sides.

Trace the triangles.

Then color in the jack-o'-lantern.

Now draw your own triangle in the space below.

How many triangles can you find?

Point to all the triangles in the picture.

Shapes and Colors

Your Star!

Do you see **a star?**

Color it yellow.

Shapes and
Colors

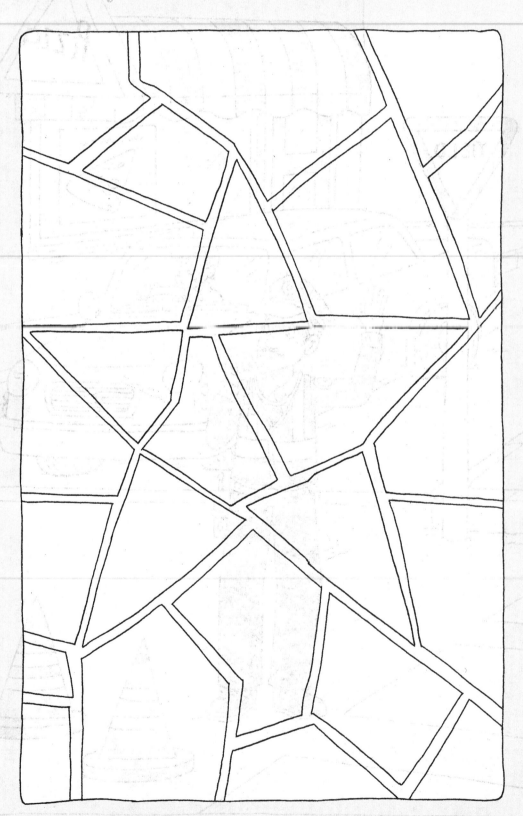

My Heart

Do you see a **heart**?

Color it red.

Cozy Quilt

Can you color the quilt?

Color the circles orange.

Color the squares green.

Color the rectangles blue.

Color the triangles **purple**.

Color the hearts **red**.

Color the stars yellow.

Kebabs!

Look at the kebabs. Do you see a pattern in the colors?

Use the pattern to help you color the last fruit on the kebab.

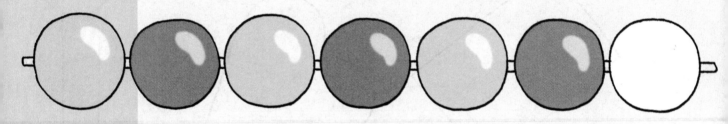

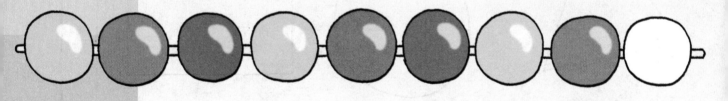

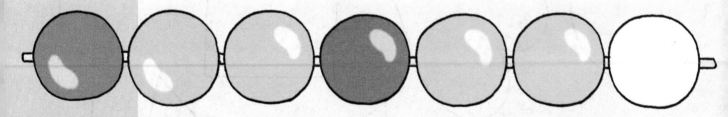

Look for the pattern in the fruit kebabs.

Circle the fruit that should go on the end
of the kebab.

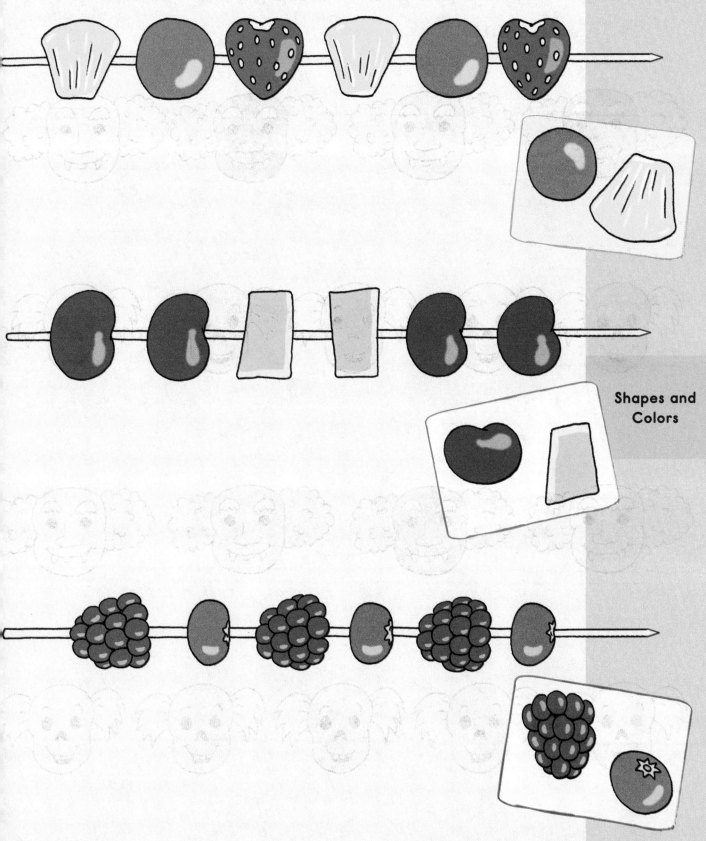

Spooky

Look at the masks. Do you see a pattern?
Use the pattern to help you color the
last mask.

Look for the pattern on the garlands.

Circle the piece that should go at the end of the garland.

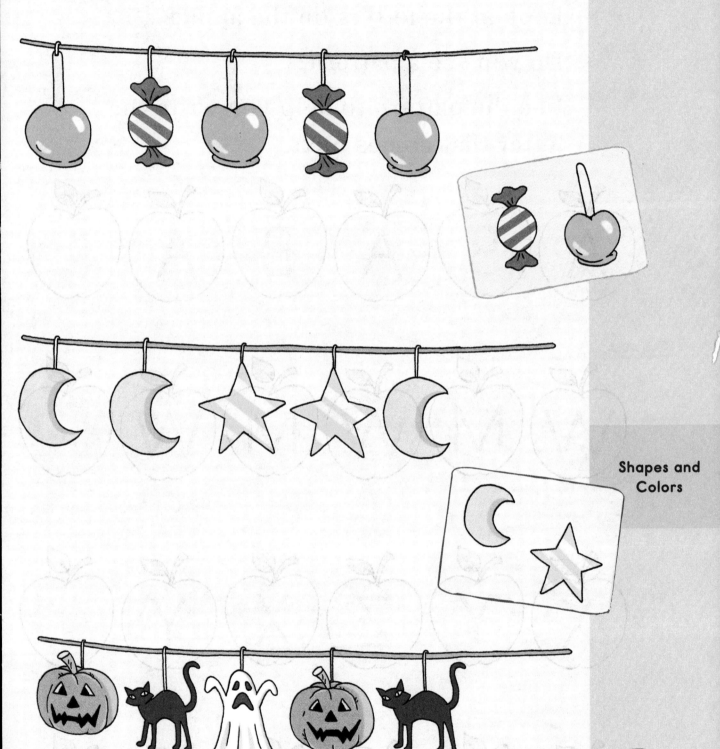

Apples

Look at the letters on the apples.

Do you see a pattern?

Use the pattern to help you write the letter that comes next.

Shapes and Colors

Sorting and Matching

Shapes

Look at each set of shapes.

Circle the two shapes that are the **same.**

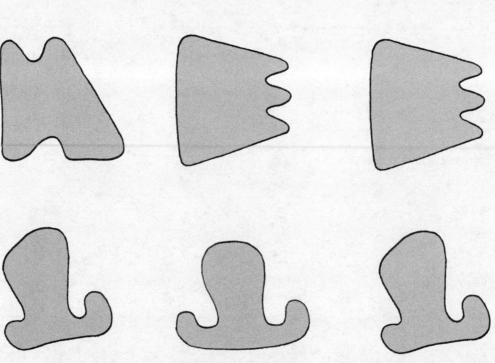

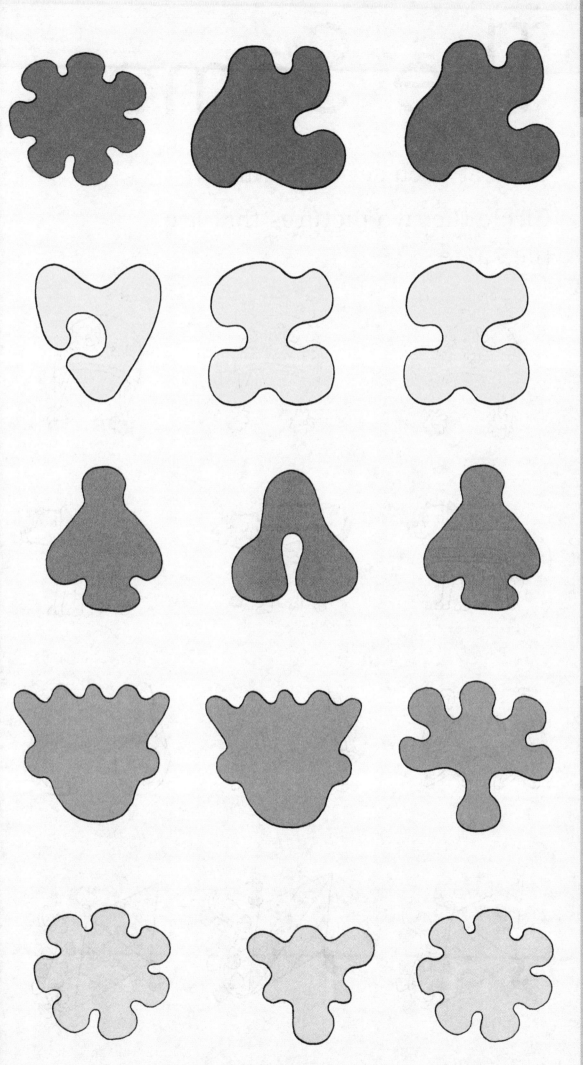

Sorting and
Matching

The Same

Look at each set of pictures.

Circle the two pictures that are the **same**.

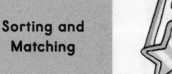

Twin Time

Twins look the **same.**

Circle the twins in each family.

Sorting and Matching

In the Sky

Look at each set of pictures.

Circle the picture that is **different**.

Sorting and Matching

It's Different

Look at each set of pictures.

Circle the picture that is **different**.

Sorting and Matching

Gum Balls!

Look at each set of gum balls.

Circle the ball that is **different**.

Sorting and
Matching

The Dragon

Look at each set of dragons.

Circle the picture that is **different**.

Art Time

Sophia is painting a picture.
Circle the two things below that
Sophia can use to paint.

Sorting and
Matching

Supper

Look at each set of pictures.

Circle the two pictures that **belong together**.

Clean Up!

Help put away these things.

Draw a line from each picture to where it belongs.

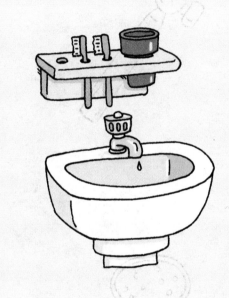

Put It Away!

Where do these things go?

Draw a line from each picture to where it belongs.

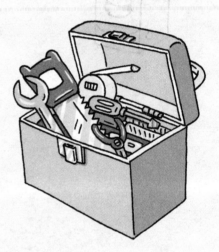

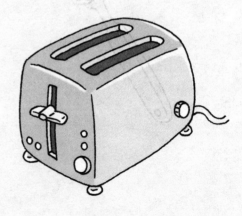

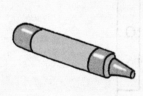

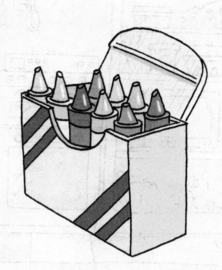

So Silly!

Something is wrong with these pictures.
Draw an X on the thing that does not belong in
each picture.

Sorting and Matching

Shoe Pairs

Two shoes that look alike make a pair.

Circle the shoe that makes a pair with the shoe on the card.

Sorting and Matching

Fly or Swim

What flies? What swims?

Circle all the things that can fly.

Draw a line under the things that can swim.

Cake!

Look at the cake.

Circle the piece that is missing.

Sorting and Matching

My World

My Home!

What happens at home?

Circle all the things you do at home.

My World

Draw a picture of your favorite thing to do at home.

My World

Dinner!

Where do these things go?

Draw a line from each small picture to where it belongs in the big picture.

My World

Kitchen!

There is a lot going on in the kitchen.
Draw a line from each small picture
to where it belongs in the big picture.

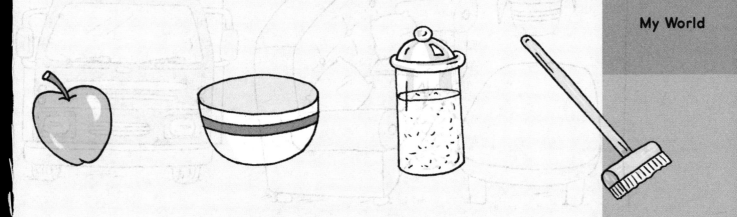

Silly House

Something is wrong with this house!

Draw an **X** on all the silly things that do not belong in the house.

My World

To School!

Children go to school many different ways.

Tell how the children go to school in each picture.

Then circle the way you go to school.

Draw a picture of you on your way to school.

At School!

What do you do at school?

Tell what the children are doing in each picture.

Then circle all the things you like to do at school.

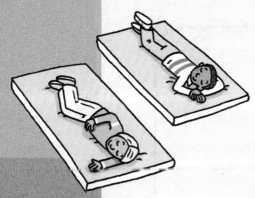

Now draw something else you like to do at school.

The Library

Look at the picture.

My World

Color the round table **red**.

Color the book about the panda **blue**.

Color the poster of the bear **brown**.

Color the poster of the lion yellow.

Color the computer green.

My World

Shopping!

This boy is shopping for a coat.

Can you tell what happens **first**?

What happens **next**?

Now point to the picture that tells what happens **last**.

Science

It's Living!

Animals are living creatures.

All living things need air, food, and water to survive.

Circle all the pictures of things that are living.

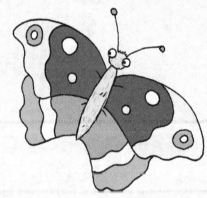

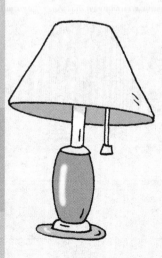

Plants!

Plants are living, too.

Most plants need water, air, and sunlight to grow.

Circle all the pictures of things that are living.

Science

Homes

Your home is where you live, eat, stay safe, and grow up.

Animals have homes, too. Animal homes are places where animals find food, stay safe, and raise their babies.

Draw a line from each animal to its home.

chicks

ants

beavers

bees

bears

beehive

underground tunnels

dam

nest

cave

Science

Habitats

A **habitat** is the place where animals live. Draw a line from each animal to its matching habitat.

fish

frog

gorilla

fox

zebra

Science

grasslands

forest

rain forest

ocean

pond

Science

The Desert

cactus

snake

coyote

The desert is hot and dry.

Draw a line from each small picture to the same thing in the big picture.

lizard

owl

fox

Science

Rain Forest

Science

snake

gorilla

parrot

It rains every day in the rain forest.

Draw a line from each small picture to the same thing in the big picture.

Science

flower

butterfly

frog

The Pond

grasshopper   fish   lily

A pond is a small lake.

Draw a line from each small picture to the same thing in the big picture.

turtle

frog

dragonfly

Undersea

Draw an X on the animals that do **not** belong in the ocean.

Song Time!

Sing "Heads, Shoulders, Knees, and Toes."

Touch the parts of your body as you sing.

Head, shoulders,
knees and toes,
knees and toes.

Head, shoulders,
knees and toes,
knees and toes,
and eyes, and ears,
and mouth, and nose.

Head, shoulders,
knees and toes,
knees and toes.

Science

head

shoulders

knees

toes

eyes

ears

mouth

nose

Science

My Body

Listen to each question.
Point to the answer on your body.

What do you use to paint and color and catch a ball?

What do you need to sit down?

What do you use to think and smile and laugh and cry?

What do you use to run and jump and kick and hop?

Where is your belly button?

Science

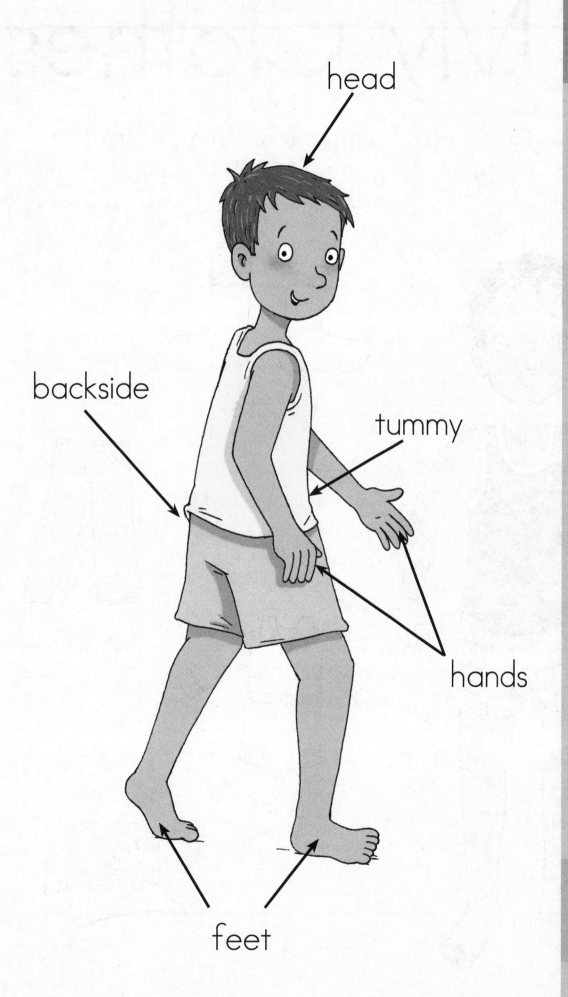

head

backside

tummy

hands

feet

My Clothes

Draw a line from each thing you wear to the part of the body it goes with.

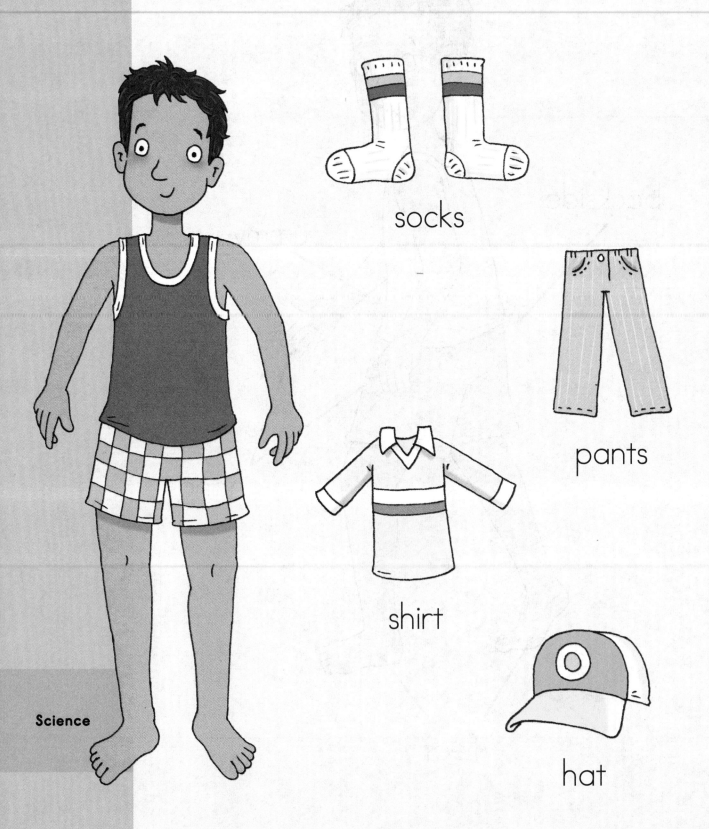

socks

pants

shirt

hat

Science

My Things

Draw a line from each thing to the
part of the body it goes with.

toothbrush
and toothpaste

glasses

hairbrush

tissues

Science

Healthy!

Boys and girls need healthy food to grow.

Name each food.

Circle the food you like to eat.

banana

apple

watermelon

orange

yogurt

grapes

cheese

milk

Science

 carrot

 tomatoes

 celery

 cucumber

 lettuce

 peas

 potato

 cereal

 pasta

 turkey

 bread

 rice

 chicken

 pork

fish

Lunchtime!

Draw your favorite meal on the plate.

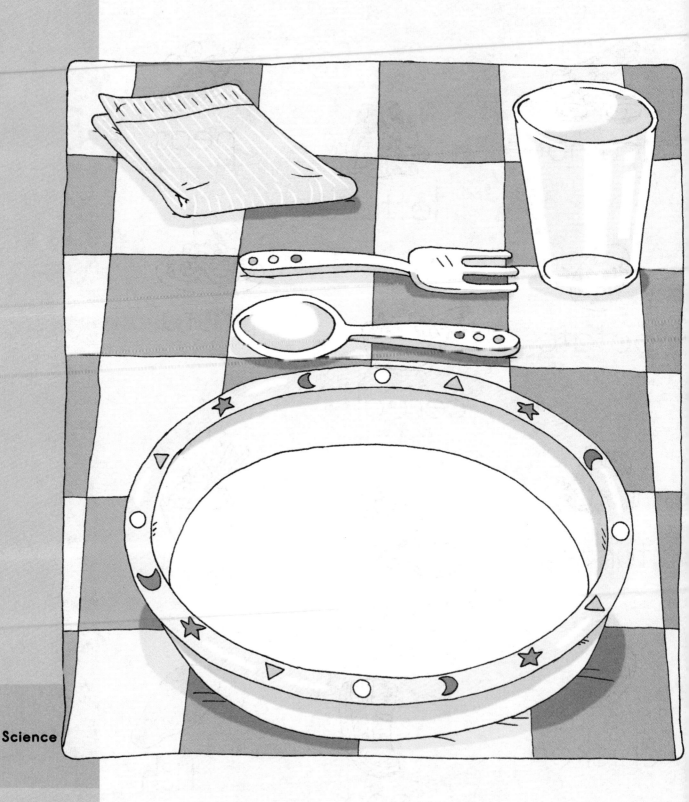

Fun and Games

Lily's Lily

Help Lily find her flower.

Ruby's Ruby

Help Ruby find her jewel.

Magic!

Help Madison find the magician.

Treasure!

The fish found the treasure!

Color the picture.

Color Me!

Find the spoon, fork, and knife.

Color them **blue**.

Then color the rest of the picture.

Find the bowl, cup, and plate.

Color them **purple**.

Then color the rest of the picture.

Fun and
Games

Dolphins!

The dolphins are playing in the water!

Color the picture.

Louie's Lost

Help Louie find his way home.

Fire Truck!

The firemen are washing the fire truck.

Color the picture.

Circus!

Help Chris the Clown get to the circus.

Penguins!

The penguins are balancing on balls!

Color the picture.

Brain Quest
Extras

Congratulations!

You've finished the Brain Quest Workbook!

In this section, you'll find:

Brain Quest Mini-Deck

Cut out the cards and make your own Brain Quest deck.

Play by yourself or with a friend.

Brainiac Certificate

Put a sticker on each square for every chapter you complete. Finish the whole workbook, and you're an official Brainiac!

And don't forget to turn to the end of the workbook. You'll find stickers and Alphabet Letters!

Questions

Find the toy that goes with each wrapped present.

Questions

Find the things that do NOT belong in the refrigerator.

Questions

Find the animal that has yellow spots.

Questions

Which picture goes with "D"?

Dd

Which picture goes with "E"?

Ee

Questions

Find the toy that goes with each wrapped present.

Questions

Which picture goes with "B"?

Bb

Which picture goes with "Q"?

Qq

Answers

Answers

Answers

Answers

Answers

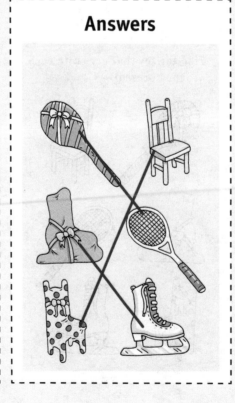

Answers

Questions

Which picture goes with "I"?

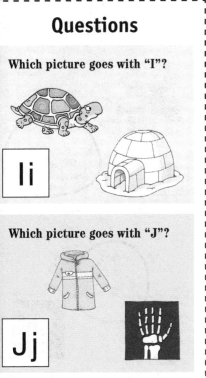

Which picture goes with "J"?

Questions

Find the animal that has a shell.

Questions

Which picture goes with "L"?

Which picture goes with "G"?

Questions

Say the word for this shape.

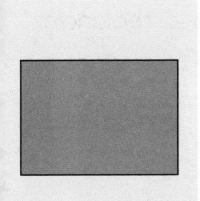

Questions

Which picture goes with "Y"?

Which picture goes with "P"?

Questions

How many stars do you see?

Answers

Answers

Answers

Answers

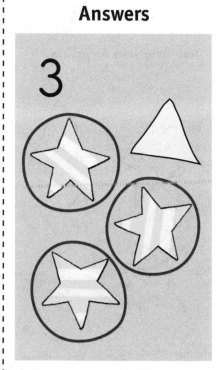

Answers

Answers

rectangle

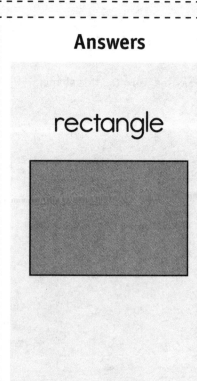

Questions

Say the word for this shape.

Questions

Which picture goes with "S"?

Ss

Which picture goes with "R"?

Rr

Questions

How many little monkeys are in the bed?

Which picture goes with "Z"?

Zz

Questions

Which picture goes with "O"?

Oo

Which picture goes with "T"?

Tt

Questions

Say the word for this shape.

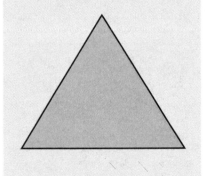

Questions

How many little monkeys are in the bed?

Which picture goes with "K"?

Kk

Answers

Answers

Answers

heart

Answers

Answers

triangle

Answers

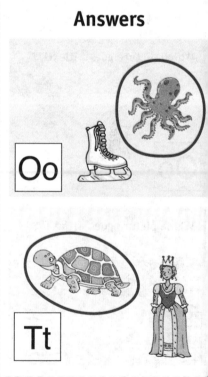

Questions

Which picture goes with "F"?

Which picture goes with "C"?

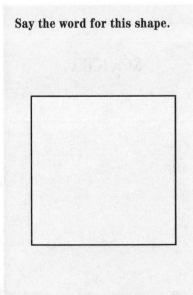

Questions

Which picture goes with "M"?

Which picture goes with "U"?

Questions

How many circles do you see?

Questions

Say the word for this shape.

Questions

Find all the carrots in the picture.

Questions

Find the musical instrument.

Answers

Answers

Answers

Answers

Answers

Answers

square

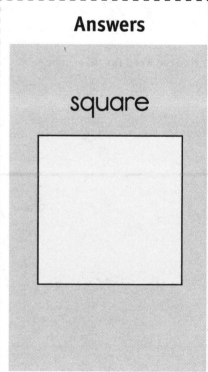

Brainiac Award!

Every time you finish a chapter of this workbook, choose a Brain Quest sticker and place it over the correct square on the certificate below. When all the squares have been covered by stickers, you will have completed the entire Brain Quest Workbook! Woo-hoo! Congratulations! That's quite an achievement.

Once you have a completed certificate, write your name on the line—or use the alphabet stickers—and cut out the award certificate.

Show your friends. Hang it on your wall! You're a certified Brainiac!

Brainiac Award

Brain Quest

Presented to:

_____

for successfully completing all nine chapters of

BRAIN QUEST PRE-K WORKBOOK

PLACE A STICKER ON EACH SQUARE AFTER YOU HAVE COMPLETED THE CHAPTER

Chapter	Chapter	Chapter	Chapter	Chapter	Chapter	Chapter	Chapter	Chapter
1	2	3	4	5	6	7	8	9

Over 28 Million Kids Can't Be Wrong!

AMERICA'S #1 EDUCATIONAL BESTSELLER

This is where it all started: the curriculum-based, fast-paced, question-and-answer series. Vetted by a panel of America's award-winning teachers and embraced by kids and parents because it flat-out works, BRAIN QUEST opens a world of information and education to kids from ages 2 to 13. IT'S FUN TO BE SMART!™

AVAILABLE WHEREVER BOOKS ARE SOLD, OR PLEASE VISIT WWW.BRAINQUEST.COM

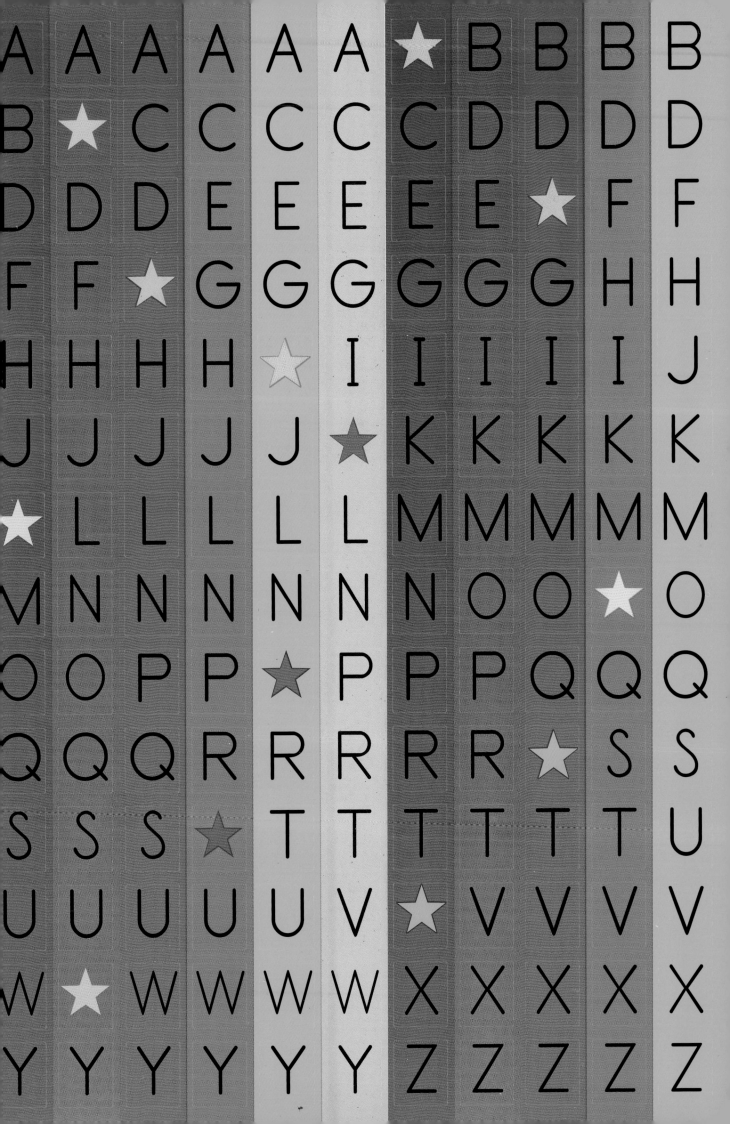

A B
F C
G D
H
I
J
K E

Alphabet Letters!
Brain Quest Pre-K Workbook